UNFAILING LOVE

Karol Ladd

UNFAILING LOVE

A Woman's Walk Through 1 John

HARVEST HOUSE PUBLISHERS
EUGENE, OREGON

Cover by Koechel Peterson & Associates, Inc., Minneapolis, Minnesota

Cover photo © iStockphoto / Thinkstock

Back-cover author photo by Shooting Starr Photography by Cindi Starr. www.shootingstarrphotos.com

UNFAILING LOVE
Copyright © 2012 by Karol Ladd
Published by Harvest House Publishers
Eugene, Oregon 97402
www.harvesthousepublishers.com

Library of Congress Cataloging-in-Publication Data
    Ladd, Karol.
    A woman's embrace of God's love / Karol Ladd.
      p. cm.
    ISBN 978-0-7369-2977-6 (pbk.)
    ISBN 978-0-7369-4269-0 (eBook)
    1. Bible. N.T. Epistle of John, 1st—Criticism, interpretation, etc. 2. Christian women—Religious life. 3. God (Christianity)—Love. I. Title.
    BS2805.52.L33 2012
    227'.9406—dc23

                                   2011046148

Printed in the United States of America

12 13 14 15 16 17 18 19 20 / VP-SK / 10 9 8 7 6 5 4 3 2 1

*To every woman who deeply desires to know true love
and is ready to allow that love to transform her life.*

Acknowledgments

A sincere thank-you to my friends at Harvest House Publishers, who share my enthusiasm for the Positive Woman Connection series. Bob, LaRae, Shane, Paul, and all those who work so tirelessly to create books founded on God's Word and that impact the world for Christ—I thank you!

I'm grateful to my agent, Steve Laube, and his continued commitment to excellence in the industry.

Tammy, Kelley, Vicki, and my wonderful husband, Curt, thank you for your encouragement along the way as I study and write.

Most importantly, I thank the Lord, who leads me and embraces me with His unfailing love each step of the way.

Contents

Divine Romance

"Immortal love, forever full,
Forever flowing free,
Forever shared, Forever whole,
A never-ebbing sea."
JOHN GREENLEAF WHITTIER

"I have loved you, my people, with an everlasting love.
With unfailing love I have drawn you to myself."
JEREMIAH 31:3 NLT

Not too long ago as I was enjoying a delightful dinner with some friends, I posed a candid question: "In your opinion, what is the greatest love story of all time?" The responses were interesting and varied—from *Jane Eyre* to *Romeo and Juliet* to *Gone with the Wind*. The romance between Queen Victoria and Prince Albert was explored. And of course *Sense and Sensibility* was also mentioned along with *Pride and Prejudice* and *Emma*—we can't leave out Jane Austen's contributions to great love stories! What about you? How would you have answered the question? Do you have a favorite true love story?

The longing for faithful and fulfilling love represents the secret yearning inside every woman's heart. Many people spend their lives trying to fill the hole in their hearts with shallow affections, unsatisfying pursuits, and less-than-perfect lovers. But there is One who will not disappoint—the Lover of Our Souls. He is true and faithful and good. Is it possible to know we are completely and dearly loved by Him? My friend, I want to assure you that you can not only know about His love, but you can *experience* the joy, strength, and comfort of His love in your daily life. As you journey along with me through the pages of this book, my hope is that you will understand the rich treasure of believing you are sincerely loved with a divine love.

The wellsprings of a woman's heart run deep. We feel emotion with intense sincerity, and we understand most people and circumstances with unique intuition. God created us with this deep insight for a purpose, and He connects with us at the heart level. When I have times of feeling misunderstood or lonely, I find great comfort in the fact that He understands my heartaches and longings with a wisdom that only "He who knows all things" could possess. As women who follow Christ, we are connected heart-to-heart with the God who formed us in our mother's womb and loves us with a faithful love that endures forever.

Maybe you don't feel loved. Please don't think you are alone. Wanting to know that we are sincerely valued and passionately desired is a cry from deep within out souls. Often the feelings of unworthiness or unloveliness stem from our thought life and are rooted in misguided concepts of ourselves or memories that continually pop up from the past. I hope that this book will help redirect your focus and help you think differently not only about yourself, but also about who God is in relationship with you.

It's easy to talk about God's love, of course, but it is another thing to embrace it, feel it, and allow it to color the fabric of your life entirely. His love is a transforming love. It changes who you are and how you see your life. It's not just something we learn about by sitting in church on Sundays—it's something very real and vibrant that affects our very being. God's love changes the way we see ourselves. Additionally, when we are flooded with the realization that we are honestly loved by the

Creator of all, it changes the way we deal with others and how we handle our closest relationships. We live and think differently about our circumstances and the people God places in our paths because we recognize we are held in the kind and loving arms of our compassionate heavenly Father.

Are you willing to explore the potential of what God's love can do in you and through you as you touch the people around you? When we allow His unchanging love to pour through us and be demonstrated in our everyday actions, we begin to make a positive difference in this world. We express His love to others through our words and actions as we ourselves experience the sincere joy of living a rich and meaningful life. Yes, we can even shine His light in dark places, brightening the world with His love.

The Words of the Beloved

In *Unfailing Love,* we will discover the joy of engaging in meaningful and lasting relationships both with God and with people. Together we are going to dig into a letter of love in the Bible, the first epistle written by John, one of Jesus' closest and dearest friends. John called himself "the disciple whom Jesus loved." He wrote this letter in order that we (fellow followers of Christ) may experience the same kind of fellowship with Christ that he did. He wrote from his own experience of being with Jesus and hearing His words. His purpose was clear—John wanted Christ's followers to be sure of who Jesus is and confident in their relationship with Him.

Could a letter that was written in the first century be relevant to your life and mine today? You bet! I think you would have to agree that the desire to love and be loved has not diminished over the centuries. People hunger for authentic love today just as much as they did thousands of years ago. John wrote about the beauty of God's love, which He lavishes upon those who believe in Christ. John proclaimed the clear truth about Christ. In a culture that leans toward viewing Jesus as a nice guy who is one of many ways to get to heaven, we need to hear John's words proclaiming loud and clear, "He who has the Son has life; he who does not have the Son of God does not have life." Yes,

I would say that John's message is just as relevant today as it was when he wrote it.

As though weaving a beautiful tapestry, John threads three themes throughout his letter so that we may have a full picture of Christ: *light, love,* and *life*. We will encounter these powerful and potent words numerous times as we examine John's letter. Think of the implications of these themes:

In our darkness, God is light.

In our loneliness, God is love.

In our dying world, God is life.

He brings meaning to our existence, joy to our spirits, victory over our discouragements, and hope to the world. Our wonderful heavenly Father cares about the details of our lives and desires to engage every aspect of them. The ultimate theme that ought to rock our world is that God cared enough to send us His Son as the Savior for our souls in order that we might have fellowship with Him.

His Story

From the beginning of time God has been writing a beautiful love story. He has chosen to generously pour out His love upon us and call us His beloved. He has rescued us and bought us with the price of His Son. My hope is that as you read this book you will experience the deep riches of His abiding love and know that His divine love was meant for you. You don't have to work for it, you don't have to strive for it—you simply receive it as a gift. His pure love compels us to be different. It motivates us to obedience and inspires us to be compassionate. The satisfaction of His redeeming love relieves us from striving to find love in unsatisfying places. The love we experience as followers of Christ goes deeper than the superficial love of people or the temporary fulfillment of things.

Because we are treasured and truly loved, we are motivated to reflect His love in all that we do. That's one of the reasons why I have added a section at the end of each chapter called "Getting Personal." In this section you will be reminded of *abiding truths*, given an *additional reading*, and shown *action steps* to help you apply the truth of God's love in your daily life. This is an inspiring book to read on your own, but you can also join with others in a group study. You will find discussion questions at the end to enhance your time together.

∽

You are about to embark on an eye-opening journey which will lead you to a greater grasp of God's love for His dear people. Honestly, I don't want this to be just another book you read; I want it to be a life-changer, a mind-grower, and a relationship-builder. Now if you were dependent on my own meager words to change your life, you would certainly be disappointed. Fortunately this book is not based on my own ideas and concepts—it is based on the timeless truths found in the Bible. I can confidently say this book has the potential to transform your life because that's what God's Word does in the lives of those who believe it and apply it.

I have never read books more simple, yet sublime.
MARTIN LUTHER,
COMMENTING ON THE EPISTLES OF JOHN

PART ONE

Living in the Light of God's Great Love

*"My soul's cry is still for more acquaintance
with the Lord Jesus,
and the Father in him."*

ANDREW BONAR

*"In the beginning was the Word,
and the Word was with God,
and the Word was God.
He was with God in the beginning.
Through him all things were made;
without him nothing was made that has been made.
In him was life, and that life was
the light of all mankind.
The light shines in the darkness,
and the darkness has not overcome it."*

THE GOSPEL OF JOHN 1:1-5

$\mathcal{C}$omplete Joy

*"God does not love us because we are valuable,
but we are valuable because God loves us."*
MARTIN LUTHER

*"I pray that you, being rooted and established in love,
may have power, together with all the Lord's holy people,
to grasp how wide and long and high
and deep is the love of Christ."*
EPHESIANS 3:17-18

When our family visited a little church on Highway 71 in the Hill Country of Texas, we didn't know quite what to expect. It was Easter Sunday and since we were out of town, we wanted to find a place to worship and discovered the delightful Pedernales River Fellowship. What we encountered was a refreshing group of people who seemed to sincerely love the Lord and care for one another's needs. The warmth and love we sensed from this body of believers was genuine. As you can imagine I was thrilled when the pastor opened up his Bible and said he was continuing with his series of sermons on 1 John. What perfect timing! I was about to embark on writing the book you have in your hands, based on 1 John, and here was a pastor preaching a whole series on the subject!

I was all ears. Pen in hand, I was ready to glean whatever I could from this rare opportunity that only God could have orchestrated. The message did not disappoint. But what I remembered most was not the sermon centering on the rich truths of God's love—rather, it was the personal story the pastor shared from his own life. With his two older kids grown and out of the house and his teenaged daughter just a few years from graduation, the pastor and his wife were ready to celebrate empty-nesthood. But God allowed Greg and Leigh Anne Bland's "nice and quiet" to be slightly interrupted with the opportunity to put His love into action.

It all started when Leigh Anne heard about a need for foster families in the Austin area to take care of some of the children who were injured in the Haitian earthquake in 2010. She attended an informational meeting and found out that the first requirement was to go through the process of foster care training as a couple. After background checks and instructional classes, Greg and Leigh Anne were quickly approved to become qualified as foster parents. But as it turned out, due to government red tape only two Haitian children came to the area, and they were already assigned to other families.

Now as you may have figured out, in God's economy nothing is ever wasted. Greg and Leigh Anne realized that there was a great need in their own area to foster abused and neglected children, and since they were already approved as foster parents they were ready to help. When they received the first call from Child Protective Services they didn't know what to expect. How would this work? How would this change their lives? The only information they were given was that they would be receiving a 21-month-old Hispanic boy who had been living in a government shelter since he was 15 months old. Young Alex was about to clock out of the system because of the statute of limitations and was in desperate need of a home.

The Blands welcomed Alex into their loving family environment, and for the first time in his short life he began to experience a caring home life. Greg and Leigh Anne still remained open to other calls. At one point they had a one-year-old, a two-year-old, and a three-year-old staying at their home all at one time. Their once orderly lives had now been turned upside down with diapers, high chairs, and strollers. Just when they thought they were done with all of this! The church family surrounded them with help and support (and diapers), and the older Bland kids also stepped up to help. In time they were back to one foster child, Alex. With his mother's rights terminated, he became available for adoption.

It was time for much contemplation and prayer for the Bland family. Greg and Leigh Anne were enjoying being at the point in their family life where they had the freedom to go out to dinner by themselves when they wanted to, or take little weekend trips now and then. Life would be different with a three-year-old son. Parent–teacher meetings, soccer practices, homework—they had to consider the possibilities as well as the details, but when it came down to the big picture, they knew they were meant to adopt Alex and couldn't bear the thought of him going back into "the system."

Although they were concerned that bringing another child into their family would take away from their own family togetherness, Greg and Leigh Anne have seen that adopting Alex has enriched and enhanced their home life and strengthened their bond as a family. Isn't that what love does? It doesn't diminish, it multiplies. Has it been tough? Sure! Sacrificial love requires an adjustment to the usual way of doing things, but in the end it is worth it. The Blands knew they were following what God had planned for their family, and now they are praying about adopting a brother or sister for Alex.[1]

This is a pastor who has not only taught from 1 John, he has actually lived it out with his family. The love of Christ is an active virtue, one that ought to play out in our daily lives. It begins as we place our faith in the living Christ and then is evidenced as we reflect His love by genuinely loving other people. Sadly, as Christians I don't think we begin to grasp how wide and deep the love of Christ is toward us, and therefore we don't actively live in that love in our daily lives. Love is action, not just words; that's what the apostle John's letter is all about.

Inside Knowledge

If you want to find out the inside scoop about another person, talk to their best friend. A friend knows what a person is like not only when everything seems to be going their way, but also when everything is falling apart. A close friend can sense authenticity and true character. John knew the real Jesus. He was one of the three disciples Jesus invited to stay close by Him and pray for Him in His darkest hour. John served with Jesus, leaned on Jesus, spoke with Jesus, and walked with Jesus. He was there at the transfiguration, the healing of the sick, the raising of the dead, and the feeding of the 5000. If you wanted to know about Jesus, John was in the inner circle and could tell you everything.

John wrote this letter, the one we are studying in this book, in order that the early believers would know the clear truth about Jesus and enjoy fellowship with Him and with each other. Doubts and speculations about both Christ's divinity and humanity were seeping into the religious-philosophical culture of the day, and John wanted to dispel false teachings as well as strengthen the believers' faith.

John especially wanted to clear up some misconceptions that were being popularized by the Gnostics. *Gnosticism* was a movement that, among other things, declared that anything of the spirit was good and anything of the flesh was evil. Obviously God is spirit and He is good, but in their belief system Jesus couldn't be both God and man because flesh is evil. John purposely emphasized Jesus' humanity as well as His deity in this letter. He had seen Jesus face-to-face. He had heard Him, he had known Him, and he had touched Him. John wanted to set the record straight so there would be no confusion.

Confusion about Christ continues today. Some think He was just a good man, while others agree He was someone special, maybe even a prophet. Some don't think about Him at all. The question we must wrestle with is, who do *we* say He is? Either He is the Son of God sent to be the Savior of the world, or He was a liar and a hoax. Jesus Himself said He came to offer life to all who believe. He came to seek and to save those who are lost. He came as God in the flesh to offer His life as a sacrifice for ours. God demonstrated His abundantly great love for us by sending His Son Jesus.

What we believe about Christ has an enormous impact on us personally. If we understand and embrace the love God has for us, it changes how we live and how we love others. John's life was transformed by Christ's love to the point that he referred to himself as the disciple whom Jesus loved.

The Beloved

Who is this disciple who so boldly claimed that he was the one Jesus loved? How could he possibly make such a claim? Was he prideful, or was he simply thankful for God's love? We meet several men named John in the New Testament (John Mark and John the Baptist being two of the others), but the author of 1 John has a unique and intriguing story. He was originally a disciple of John the Baptist, but when he met Jesus he began to follow Him. John and his brother James were a part of Jesus' core group along with Peter. Jesus allowed these three to join Him during the transfiguration, and He asked them to stay close to Him as He agonized over the coming cross in the Garden of Gethsemane.

I don't believe John called himself the beloved disciple from a standpoint of arrogance, but rather a place of humility. He truly experienced and embraced the love Christ had for him. He understood it, received it, lived it, breathed it in a way few people actually do. His deep love for God was born out of his recognition that he was sincerely loved.

Not too long ago a friend of mine attended a funeral of a respected businessman and devoted family man who had died of cancer. At the funeral each of his three teenage children came up to the pulpit to share a few words, and each one said they instinctively felt as though they were the favorite child. They sincerely felt their father's love almost to the point of thinking it was meant only for them. This father obviously did a great job of showing his kids he loved them. They understood it and received it. In the same way, our heavenly Father lavishes His love upon each of us as His children, and I believe John received it and accepted it to the point that he thought in a humble way that he was most loved.

We too can know and experience the rich love that comes from having fellowship with the Father. Paul identified believers as "holy and dearly loved." In other words, we are His beloved. We are His bride, set apart for Him. I hope that as we study this book together, you will find yourself thinking, *I'm one of His favorites. I'm sincerely loved by Him.* I don't want you to think of it in a prideful sense—rather, think of it in all humility. Recognizing you are a sinner and receiving His grace-filled love, you know you are deeply and completely loved. Yes, you are His beloved daughter, the one He loves, and so am I!

Perhaps John recognized God's great love for him because he also recognized his own personal sin nature. Jesus called John and his brother James "Sons of Thunder." As fishermen in their father's business, James and John seemed to both be ambitious and a bit judgmental. In Mark's Gospel we read the story of their boldness in asking for a place of honor in God's kingdom:

> *James and John, the sons of Zebedee, came to him. "Teacher," they said, "we want you to do for us whatever we ask."*
>
> *"What do you want me to do for you?" he asked.*
>
> *They replied, "Let one of us sit at your right and the other at your left in your glory."*
>
> *"You don't know what you are asking," Jesus said. "Can you drink the cup I drink or be baptized with the baptism I am baptized with?"*
>
> *"We can," they answered.*
>
> *Jesus said to them, "You will drink the cup I drink and be baptized with the baptism I am baptized with, but to sit at my right or left is not for me to grant. These places belong to those for whom they have been prepared."[2]*

Jesus used this as an opportunity to teach that if you want to be a leader in God's kingdom, learn to be a servant. Oh, ouch! Looks like John had a little learning and maturing to do as a disciple of Christ.

Another place we read about John and his brother is in the Gospel of Luke. Here we get an idea of the slightly judgmental spirit John had in his heart.

> *As the time approached for him to be taken up to heaven, Jesus resolutely set out for Jerusalem. And he sent messengers on ahead, who went into a Samaritan village to get things ready for him; but the people there did not welcome him, because he was heading for Jerusalem. When the disciples James and John saw this, they asked, "Lord, do you want us to call fire down from heaven to destroy them?" But Jesus turned and rebuked them. Then he and his disciples went to another village.* [3]

Did you catch that Jesus turned and rebuked the brothers? Oops! So maybe John and his brother James had a few mistaken ideas now and then. Don't we all? What do you do with your mistakes? Do you review them and think about them and beat yourself up over them? Sadly, most of us as women tend to rehearse old, stupid stuff we said or did in the past. Let's learn to move on. If God used John in mighty ways, He can use us despite our mistakes and mess-ups as well. Remember, John saw himself as the disciple whom Jesus loved, maybe because he recognized the love Jesus had for him looked past the mistakes and saw his heart. It is interesting to note that John remained at the foot of the cross on Calvary with Jesus' mother Mary and later took her into his care. One who was "much loved" showed much love. Never underestimate the transforming power of Christ's love in our lives!

By the time John wrote his first epistle to the early believers he was an elderly man. God had taught him and caused him to mature over his years as a disciple and an early church leader. It is believed that John was the oldest living disciple at the time of the writing of 1 John and most likely was in his late eighties or early nineties. He wrote his Gospel between AD 80 and 90, with the purpose of showing conclusively that Jesus is the Son of God and that all who believe in Him have eternal life. John then wrote his epistles with the aim of reassuring believers in their faith, encouraging their life in Christ, and also countering false teachings. He wanted believers to know that in Christ alone they experience true love.

John lived in Ephesus at the time he wrote his Gospel and the three epistles. Tertullian (lived about AD 160–220), an early Christian author and apologist, recorded an incredible story about John that took place during the reign of Domitian, a first-century Roman emperor. Known for his persecution of Christians, Domitian sentenced John to be plunged into boiling oil. Yet, to the amazement of the crowds in the Roman Coliseum, John was miraculously preserved and not harmed in any way. Since he didn't die, Domitian banished him to the island of Patmos, where he eventually wrote Revelation. It is said that many in the crowd that day believed in Christ as a result of witnessing this miracle. John went on to live to an old age, and it is believed that he died of natural causes.

Touchable

Unapproachable, unknowable, untouchable. That's how we could describe the lives of most of the rich, famous, and powerful people in our culture today, whether we are talking about notable athletes, Hollywood celebrities, or important politicians. With prominence comes isolation from the public and a guarded distance from "normal people"—and understandably so. But that is not how God is toward us. He deliberately allowed Himself to be approachable, knowable, and touchable. What a magnificent truth! Whereas the Gnostics believed that only an exclusive, elite group had the privilege of having special spiritual insight and wisdom, John wanted everyone to have the special knowledge of knowing Christ, so he began his letter in this way:

1 JOHN 1:1-2

That which was from the beginning, which we have heard, which we have seen with our eyes, which we have looked at and our hands have touched—this we proclaim concerning the Word of life. The life appeared; we have seen it and testify to it, and we proclaim to you the eternal life, which was with the Father and has appeared to us.

Notice there were no formal greetings or introductions in this letter. No identification of the writer or the recipients of the letter, unlike most of the epistles in the New Testament. John just jumps right in there with the truth. He's a get-down-to-business type of guy, and I like that about him. No wonder Jesus called him and his brother "Sons of Thunder." Both James and John tended to strike quickly and boldly with the truth. You may recognize that the Gospel of John starts out in a similar fashion: "In the beginning was the Word, and the Word was with God, and the Word was God."

Why does John call Jesus the Word (*logos*) of life? What significance is there to that title? Think about the power of our words. They reveal our thoughts and let people know what is going on inside of our hearts. Our words communicate the essence of who we are. In a similar way, Jesus revealed who God is. He communicated God to the world. Just as God used words to speak all of creation into existence, Jesus (the Word) brought salvation into existence. He is the Word of Life. He was there at the creation of life, and through Him we have eternal life.

"In the beginning" is used several different times and in several different ways in Scripture. Most of us recognize the words from Genesis: "In the beginning God created the heavens and the earth." Obviously this refers to the beginning of creation of the universe. Yet, in John's *Gospel* we read, "In the beginning was the Word." This "beginning" refers to the eternity before the universe was created, for there the Word (Jesus) existed with God and was God. As we look into John's *epistle* we see a third type of "In the beginning," which refers to the beginning of Christianity, and Christ's life here on earth. I know that may seem like a small detail, but it will help us in our understanding of John's letter.

John says, "The life appeared." In other words the life was revealed or was made manifest or known. John proclaims that he has seen, heard, and touched this life that appeared. He knew that this life was real and that Jesus was human and here in the flesh. John wasn't speaking about Christ just out of hearsay like some of the false teachers, who had never met Jesus personally. John could say with confidence that he had touched Jesus. In these few short verses he declares both Jesus' humanity and deity. Notice he calls Jesus the eternal life that was "with the Father and has appeared to us." There is only one who is eternal, and that is God Himself. Yes, Jesus is both God and man. John experienced Him, and he wanted all of us as his readers to experience Him as well.

Common Grounds

In Waco, Texas, there is a coffee shop that's always brimming with people. It's called Common Grounds. Baylor students go there to study, Waco locals hang out there to chat, and just about every weekend there is a benefit concert of some sort to raise funds for local causes as well as those abroad. It's a great place for people of all different walks of life to come together and enjoy common ground. John wanted the early believers to come together based on the common ground of knowing Christ. He used the word *fellowship* to express this unique and divine common ground.

Here's what he said:

1 JOHN 1:3-4

We proclaim to you what we have seen and heard, so that you also may have fellowship with us. And our fellowship is with the Father and with his Son, Jesus Christ. We write this to make our joy complete.

Fellowship in today's vocabulary seems to be a "Christiany" word. Most churches have a fellowship hall, a fellowship dinner, or some sort of after-church fellowship. All of these seem to have a vague sense of a gathering of some sort, often revolving around food, which is probably one of the reasons I like this word. Yet in its truest form, what does the word *fellowship* really mean? Well, it is much more than an event hall at your local church—it is actually a word rich with meaning and packed with potential.

The Greek word for *fellowship* is *koinonia,* and it conveys the idea of a partnership. It refers to people who possess something in common and partake in it together—a coming together or joining together for one purpose. I've often heard it said, "You can remember what fellowship means by picturing two fellows in a ship." One of the many purposes of John's letter was to enrich the common bond between believers and to encourage their fellowship with Christ.

It's interesting to me to see the types of common interests that seem to bring people together in our culture today. If you check out some of the Facebook groups, you begin to see that people join together over the most peculiar things. Here are a few of the oddest groups I've come across, each with a huge amount of members. With which of the following groups do you share a common bond?

- People Who Always Have to Spell Their Names for Other People
- Those Who Have Ever Pushed a Pull Door (and wouldn't that be all of us?)
- When I Was Your Age, Pluto Was a Planet (This will soon hit the one million member mark on Facebook if it hasn't already.)
- If I Fail My Exam, It's Facebook's Fault
- I Will Go out of My Way to Step on a Leaf If It Looks Particularly Crunchy
- I Use My Cell Phone to See in the Dark
- Kids Who Hid in Clothing Racks While Their Parents Were Shopping
- Students Against Backpacks with Wheels
- I Flip My Pillow Over to Get to the Cold Side

Facebook is evidence in itself that we all want to connect and experience some sort of camaraderie. But virtual connection can't replace the true *koinonia* of believers in the common bond of Christ. As believers we have a heart connection based on our common love in the Lord. This kind of connection draws us together deeply because the common bond is based on the Word of life, the One who is truth and has redeemed us. May we all recognize the value of this authentic connection and pursue it with joy.

True fellowship among Christians is not simply something we do in order to have more friends; it is also something we need. As believers we are strengthened by each other as we encourage each other from God's Word and pray for one another. At the time John wrote this letter, the early believers were experiencing persecution. Many had lost their work or had been taken off to prison, and some had even been executed. Believers needed to come together to help and strengthen one another. Although we may not be facing significant daily persecution as the early believers did (although we don't want to ignore the fact that many are persecuted in other countries), we still need fellowship with one another.

Sincere Christian fellowship can help keep us from straying from the faith or being distracted by false teachings and beliefs. The writer of Hebrews said,

> *Let us consider how we may spur one another on toward love and good deeds, not giving up meeting together, as some are in the habit of doing, but encouraging one another—and all the more as you see the Day approaching.* [4]

How deliberate are you about coming together with fellow believers to encourage and strengthen one another? John Phillips spoke of the importance of our common grounds in this way: "Fellowship is a tender plant. It must be nurtured and cared for and protected, or it can easily wither and die." [5]

Authentic fellowship takes intentional effort on our part. Do not just wait for someone to come to you, take the time to reach out to others. This coming together of believers can happen in simple ways, whether through a life group at a church or a prayer group in an organization. I'm a part of a group called Christian Women in Media Association. This organization is blessed with members all over the globe, and as a leadership team we come together in fellowship through regular prayer calls.

I can't tell you what a blessing it is to meet together over the airwaves to pray together on a conference call from all our various locations. It bonds us. It develops a deeper love for the Lord and for each other. I must admit that there was a time when I didn't make the regular prayer call a priority in my life, and I missed out. When I made the deliberate decision to be on the call whenever I could, my heart was strengthened tremendously by the fellowship of my sisters in Christ. Fellowship is worth the effort.

Partnering with God

Notice that John described an even deeper fellowship—the fellowship he had with the Father and with His Son, Jesus Christ. Oh, how amazing to think that we can fellowship with the God of all creation and with the Savior of the world! When we think of fellowship in its truest sense then we recognize that as Christians we come together with God in a partnership, working together for a common goal. It just stirs me up in my heart to think that God wants to partner with us to do His work for His kingdom. What a high calling! What a privilege! What a blessing!

Our fellowship with God begins when we place our faith in Christ. Sinful man cannot have fellowship with a holy God unless there is a mediator. Jesus is the one who bridged the gap, and because of what He did on the cross, we are able to have fellowship with the Father.

The word *partnership* makes me think of business partners—two people who have come together to run a successful organization, each one doing his or her part in conjunction with the other for the common goal of furthering their business. Partnership also makes me think about a marriage partnership, a man and a wife who love each other. In a perfect scenario, they work joyfully together building their marriage and their family and hopefully making a positive difference in the world as they serve together. In a similar way, God partners with us to be fruitful and bless the people we encounter day in and day out.

God never intended for us to work alone. Jesus said, "I am the vine; you are the branches. If you remain in me and I in you, you will bear much fruit; apart from me you can do nothing."[6] The word *remain* refers to dwelling with or abiding with someone. Fellowship! Yes, the most significant fellowship in our lives is with God. As we abide with Him and meet with Him each day, we grow to experience a satisfaction in our soul and a peace in our hearts that the world cannot duplicate. Fellowshipping with God happens in a significant way during the quiet time we have alone with Him. This is where the hunger of our hearts finds nourishment and joy. This is where we discover meaning and purpose…by partnering with God.

How easy it is to wander on our own, trying to make sense of our lives. How fruitless our days become when we ignore beautiful fellowship with the Father. His invitation has always been, "Come! Come abide with Me, find your rest in Me, discover your purpose with Me, walk together with Me." John knew the joy of fellowship with the Father, and he recognized that his joy would be fulfilled by seeing every believer experience this same kind of fellowship. Fellowship with one another is born out of fellowship with the Father. Because we love Him, we love His people.

Perfect Partnership

On the first Friday of every month, hundreds of women flock together to a movie theater in Southlake, Texas, to listen to a speaker share on topics pertinent to women's lives. Lisa Rose started "First Friday" several years ago in an effort to draw together the women in her community within the common bond of finding hope in God.[7] Her leadership team is made up of women who describe themselves as having received hope, help, and a hand up from God and from other women—they simply want to pass on to others what they themselves have received. How did this dynamic event begin? It began with Lisa's partnership with God.

Lisa is a woman of prayer, and she deeply loves the Lord. She spends time in fellowship with Him in prayer and loves studying and growing in His Word. One day she was praying specifically about what God wanted her to do for the women in her area because someone had asked her, "What gift has God given you that you need to re-gift to someone else?" As she prayed, God gave her a creative idea to start an event where women of all denominations could come together to hear a different speaker each month. The title "First Friday" popped into her head as well. Now Lisa was already a busy woman, but she knew that where God guides, He provides.

He has led her every step of the way, providing a helpful team of women and direction she needs to plan and build this delightful event, and surrounding her with a committed leadership team. She finds great joy in providing a venue where people can connect with the One who loves them most. After God and her family, Lisa's passion is to see people discover who God is, who He created them to be, and what His purpose is for their lives. Never underestimate what can happen as you fellowship with the Father and watch Him work in the fellowship between you and other believers.

Dear friend, recognize you are in partnership with the Father to carry out His will here on earth. You have a high calling and important work to do here. Meet with Him each day. Abide with Him in prayer. Meditate on His Word. Allow Him to guide you along the path you are to go. He is the eternal God, and He has created you for a purpose. Enjoy the partnership and rejoice in true fellowship with both Him and other believers.

Getting Personal

ABIDING TRUTHS:

- Jesus is the Word of Life and Eternal Life.

- Jesus is fully man and is fully God.

- Fellowship with believers gives us encouragement and strength.

- We are in partnership with God. He has a plan and a purpose for us.

- There is great joy in fellowship with God and with believers. Be deliberate about both.

- Be open to ways God wants to use you to affect others.

ADDITIONAL READING: The first chapter of the Gospel of John

ACTION STEPS: Intentional fellowship

Consider the depth of fellowship you are currently enjoying in your life and evaluate if you need to be more intentional about strengthening the common bonds you experience in your life with other believers and with God.

Fellowship with the Father

How would you describe your partnership with God right now? _____
_____
_____

What is one intentional step you can take to fellowship with Him on a deeper level? _____
_____

Fellowship with other believers

How would you describe the fellowship you have with other believers right now? _____
_____
_____

What is one way I can make an effort to strengthen the common bonds between other believers and me?_____
_____
_____

$\mathcal{L}$ight Up Your Life

*"Unless God's Word illumine the way,
the whole of life of men is wrapped in darkness and mist,
so that they cannot but miserably stray."*
John Calvin

*"In him was life, and that life
was the light of all mankind.
The light shines in the darkness,
and the darkness has not overcome it."*
John 1:4-5

When I was a science teacher I was always fascinated by the spectrum of light and the rainbow of colors that appears when light is refracted. Whether it is a rainbow in the sky, a sunset, a puddle, a prism, or cut glass on a chandelier, refracted light always reveals the same order of colors: red, orange, yellow, green, blue, indigo, violet. In my classroom, I used the acrostic "Roy G. Biv" to help the kids remember the order of colors. The spectrum of color is consistent and you can always depend on it being exactly in the same order. It never changes!

Isn't it interesting how many of the characteristics of light seem to reflect certain attributes of God? Just as the spectrum of light is unchangeable, so our glorious God is immutable and unchangeable. The Bible says, "Every good and perfect gift is from above, coming down from the Father of the heavenly lights, who does not change like shifting shadows."[1]

It's no wonder that John used the metaphor of light to describe God. God is light and in Him is no darkness at all. Darkness can't overtake light, but light drives out or dispels darkness. I don't know about you, but I definitely feel safer in the light. Law-enforcement officers agree that one of the greatest deterrents to criminal activity is the presence of light. Darkness is not compatible with light—the two cannot co-exist. Light is also revealing. There are times when I think I've cleaned the countertops in my kitchen fairly well, but when the bright morning sunlight pours through the windows, I see smudges and dirt I never knew existed. In a similar way, as God shines His light into my life, I not only feel the warmth of His love, but I can see some areas that may need to be cleaned up as well.

In the Old Testament God used a pillar of fire that gave light to illuminate the darkness as the Israelites progressed through the wilderness on their way to the Promised Land. Light brightens a dark pathway, allowing us to see the steps ahead. I remember as a camp counselor how dependent I was on my flashlight at night to lead my campers back to our cabin. The Bible says that God's Word is a lamp for our feet and a light for our path. In Scripture we read not only that God is light, but that His Word is a light that guides our steps in this dark world.

I think about how many times I've been discouraged or down and have looked to the light of God's Word to remind me of His compassionate love and care. I remember a particular time when I was in college and I was feeling down for some reason (probably something monumental like a boyfriend breakup). I happened to open my Bible to Psalm 103, and the light of God's love poured into my heart and warmed my soul with His comfort: "Praise the LORD, my soul, and forget not all his benefits—who forgives all your sins and heals all your diseases, who redeems your life from the pit and crowns you with love and compassion." I remember this was one of the first times in my life I experienced the palpable and true sense of soothing and comfort that can radiate only from the light of God's Word.

Scientists throughout the centuries have studied light, but there is so much yet to be discovered about its characteristics. One current debate concerns where light came from in the beginning. Where and how did it originate? The Bible tells us that light originated from God. In Genesis we read, "God said, 'Let there be light,' and there was light." The Creator of light is the Light of the world.

The Manifestation of Light

Often in Scripture, light refers to holiness and purity, while darkness refers to evil and sin. God is completely holy and represents absolute purity. There is no sin in Him, not even the smallest portion. Darkness is a place where things are hidden, but when God shines His light in our lives, He not only reveals sin and dispels darkness, He grants us wisdom. He opens our eyes to see things we may have never seen before. He lights up our spiritual eyes to see. David said that in God's light we see light. If we are walking in fellowship with the God who is Light, then we too are in the light.

One of my favorite devotionals is entitled *Morning and Evening,* by Charles Haddon Spurgeon. In this insightful work, Spurgeon wrote short devotional thoughts based on single verses of Scripture, one for the morning and one for the evening of each day. A devotion that particularly stood out to me focused on Christ as the light of heaven, based on Revelation 21:23: "The city does not need the sun or the moon to shine on it, for the glory of God gives it light, and the Lamb is its lamp." Here are Spurgeon's thoughts (keep in mind that this was written in the late 1800s):

> Quietly contemplate the Lamb as the light of heaven. Light in Scripture is the emblem of joy. The joy of the saints in heaven is comprised in this: Jesus chose us, loved us, bought us, cleansed us, robed us, kept us, glorified us: we are here entirely through the Lord Jesus. Each one of these

thoughts shall be to them like a cluster of the grapes of Eshcol. Light is also the cause of beauty. Naught of beauty is left when light is gone. Without light no radiance flashes from the sapphire, no peaceful ray proceedeth from the pearl; and thus all the beauty of the saints above comes from Jesus. As planets, they reflect the light of the Sun of Righteousness; they live as beams proceeding from the central orb.

If He withdrew, they must die; if His glory were veiled, their glory must expire. Light is also the emblem of knowledge. In heaven our knowledge will be perfect, but the Lord Jesus Himself will be the fountain of it. Dark providences, never understood before, will then be clearly seen, and all that puzzles us now will become plain to us in the light of the Lamb. Oh! what unfoldings there will be and what glorifying of the God of love!

Light also means manifestation. Light manifests. In this world it doth not yet appear what we shall be. God's people are a hidden people, but when Christ receives His people into heaven, He will touch them with the wand of His own love, and change them into the image of His manifested glory. They were poor and wretched, but what a transformation! They were stained with sin, but one touch of His finger, and they are bright as the sun, and clear as crystal.

Oh! what a manifestation! All this proceeds from the exalted Lamb. Whatever there may be of effulgent splendour, Jesus shall be the centre and soul of it all. Oh! to be present and to see Him in His own light, the King of kings, and Lord of lords!

We can look forward to that day when the glorious radiance of God provides light for the new heaven and the new earth. His light is all we will need, and there will be no darkness. In our present state there is darkness around us, but if we walk in the light as He is in the light we need not fear the darkness. May we bask in the radiance of His love as He lights our paths and guides our way through this dark world.

> *Praise you, Light of the world. Thank You for the warmth of Your love and the light of Your wisdom. Continue to lead me and guide me along Your way. Shine Your light on the dark corners of my life and create in me a clean spirit. Help me to shine Your light so that others may know Your love.*

Walk in the Light

In high school it wasn't too difficult to figure out who belonged to which group. The athletes were always easy to spot because of their letter jackets and confident demeanor, and they always ate together at what was known as the "jock table." Then there were the study nerds, who always hung out in the library and had their calculators in their pockets or strapped to their belts. The mean girls positioned themselves together each morning at one end of the hall so they could hold court and gossip about everyone walking to their lockers. Aren't you glad you aren't still in high school?

In life, we tend to have certain identifying factors that relate us to certain groups. When it comes to those who walk in the light and those who walk in the darkness, there are also identifying factors. Here's how John put it:

1 JOHN 1:5-7

This is the message we have heard from him and declare to you: God is light; in him there is no darkness at all. If we claim to have fellowship with him and yet walk in the darkness, we lie and do not live out the truth. But if we walk in the light, as he is in the light, we have fellowship with one another, and the blood of Jesus, his Son, purifies us from all sin.

The word "walk" implies how someone lives their life. Think for a moment what it means to live in darkness. There is secrecy in the darkness, hidden evil and deception. To live in the darkness one must stay away from the light, not wanting to identify or illuminate the sin lurking within. In darkness there is spiritual blindness and we are not able to see the truth. To walk or live in the light, on the other hand, means being genuine and honest about who we are—not perfect, but rather recognizing our need for a Savior. It means acknowledging our dependence on Christ and stepping into God's truth. If we are walking in the light then we are walking in fellowship with Him.

What does it mean to walk in the light in practical terms? The apostle Paul wrote specifically about this in his letter to the Ephesians:

> *Follow God's example, therefore, as dearly loved children and walk in the way of love, just as Christ loved us and gave himself up for us as a fragrant offering and sacrifice to God.*
>
> *But among you there must not be even a hint of sexual immorality, or of any kind of impurity, or of greed, because these are improper for God's holy people. Nor should there be obscenity, foolish talk or coarse joking, which are out of place, but rather thanksgiving...*
>
> *For you were once darkness, but now you are light in the Lord. Live as children of light (for the fruit of the light consists in all goodness, righteousness and truth) and find out what pleases the Lord. Have nothing to do with the fruitless deeds of darkness, but rather expose them. It is shameful even to mention what the disobedient do in secret.*
>
> *But everything exposed by the light becomes visible—and everything that is illuminated becomes a light. This is why it is said:*
>
> > *"Wake up, sleeper,*
> > *rise from the dead,*
> > *and Christ will shine on you."*[2]

Paul didn't want followers of Christ to be associated with the deeds of darkness. He wanted believers to walk in the light, live in the light, and shine Christ's light. Light wakes us up out of our sleep. Let us not be sleeping Christians who say one thing and yet live another way. Instead, we must be diligent to live in the light of God's truth and walk in close fellowship with God.

Recently we took our dogs with us on a trip out to the country, an area near some ranch land in the hill country of Texas. Normally we keep them safe in the yard where we're staying, but one night our mastiff, Angel, decided to run out into the dark night to chase a deer. Curt jumped into the car to look for her while I kept calling out into the darkness, "Angel! Angel! Come!" It was dangerous for her to be alone in the dark. We had heard packs of coyotes howling every night, and there was a busy, poorly lighted road nearby. Angel is also on special medication for Addison's disease and would not be able to survive without it. The darkness was perilous to her, and I felt so helpless standing at the edge of the lighted path, calling out into the black of the night.

Getting no response, I decided to move to the front of the house. Now feeling somewhat frantic, I resumed calling her. As I stood at the edge of the darkness, yelling from the little spot of light beaming from the frontporch, I saw a shape emerge. Walking slowly, Angel stepped out of the darkness and into the safety of the light and my warm embrace! She was finally safe at home with her master, who cared for her needs. It was a picture to me of what John is portraying with his analogy of light and darkness. In spiritual darkness there are loneliness, danger, fears, and temptations. But when we step into the light of God's truth, as we place our faith in Christ, everything changes. We are never alone. We are loved and cared for by our faithful and kind Lord and Master, Jesus Christ.

His invitation to us is "Come." As we come to Him a transformation takes place. We step into the light of His love, and we no longer live in spiritual darkness. We walk in fellowship with our Master, who loves us and gave His life for us. The darkness holds no power over us. We can never be lost in spiritual darkness again because His light is in us. He lights our path and allows us to see. Jesus, the Light of the world, told us, His followers, to let our lights shine before men so they may see our good works and glorify the Lord. May our lights shine brightly in this dark world!

Stain Remover

In my opinion, one of the most beautiful phrases in John's epistle is "The blood of Jesus, his Son, purifies us from all sin." We who are stained with sin are made pure and clean by His blood. Now to the Gnostics this was abhorrent, because blood represented the flesh and of course was evil. Yet John is telling us that it is the blood of Christ that purifies us, which probably really ruffled the Gnostics' feathers.

In the Old Testament, the Israelites offered blood sacrifices to cover their sins before God. Year after year on the Day of Atonement they would offer up sacrifices to cover their sins once again. The blood only covered their sins; it didn't get rid of them completely. Think of it this way—if you have ever spilled grape or cranberry juice on a light-colored carpet, you know the extreme challenge of getting rid of the stain. There have been times when we have literally rearranged an entire room to cover up such a stain! Been there? The Old Testament sacrifices temporarily covered the sin problem, but Jesus' blood does not just cover our sin problem—it purifies us from all sin. It gets the stain out!

The penalty of our sin is completely removed by the only cleanser that would work—the holy and sinless blood of Christ. Did you notice the word *all*? To draw on the words of the hymn "It Is Well with My Soul," our sin, "not in part, but the whole, is nailed to the cross" and we "bear it no more"! When we placed our faith in Christ, He took away all our sin. That doesn't mean we don't sin—it means that we do not bear the guilt or penalty of our sin. God sees us as clean and forgiven. Before we trusted Christ we were sinners, but now God sees us as forgiven. In Colossians we read, "He has reconciled you by Christ's physical body through death to present you holy in his sight, without blemish and free from accusation."[3] He has rescued us from our sin problem, from the dominion of darkness, and brought us into the kingdom of light.

John makes it clear that we can't say we have fellowship with God, and still continue to walk in sinful ways. There ought to be evidence of our life in Christ. If we are following Christ and walking in His ways, we will have beautiful fellowship with Him. Just as a rebellious kid distances himself from the close relationship he had with his parents, so when we live in habitual or continual sin we are, simply put, lying if we say we have close fellowship with the Father.

The Greatest Deception

In 1998 a movie called *The Truman Show* hit the big screen. Jim Carrey starred as Truman Burbank, a run-of-the-mill businessman who was unaware he was living in a gigantic constructed reality television show that was broadcast around the clock to people all over the world. The viewers of the show watched Truman as he grew up in a simple seacoast town. They watched him eating breakfast, playing ball, going to school, and eventually getting married and going to work. Unbeknownst to him, all the people he encountered in his daily activities were really actors on the set. Eventually Truman begins to discover that his life has been a fake all along. He finally brings the truth to light and uncovers the deception, bringing the broadcast production to a screeching halt.

No one likes to be deceived. *The Truman Show* is fictional, but there are very real deceptions in our world that can keep us from seeing the truth. When it comes to how we stand before God, here are some deceptions that are prevalent:

- Everybody is basically good.
- I'm pretty good. I mean, my good outweighs my bad.
- I'm not a sinner. A murderer or a thief or a rapist is a sinner, but not me. I do a lot of good things.

Ignoring or downplaying our sin has been Satan's lie from the beginning. He whispers in our ears, "Your sin is not that bad." In John's day there were apparently two teachings that were both false and were causing confusion among believers. One was that believers could maintain a sinful lifestyle and still have fellowship with God. The Gnostics suggested that since only spirit was good, what was done in the flesh didn't really matter. John boldly and clearly confronted this line of thought by calling it a lie: "If we claim to have fellowship with him and yet walk in the darkness, we lie and do not live out the truth."

The other false teaching was almost the opposite. The do-gooders claimed that they did not sin at all and therefore walked with God in moral perfection. The Pharisees in Jesus' time were over-the-top rule-followers. They thought they were perfect because they kept all of the laws. Yet Jesus knew their hearts. In the Sermon on the Mount He said, "Blessed are the poor in spirit, for theirs is the kingdom of heaven."[4] He was saying, blessed are those who recognize the poverty of their own souls and their need for a Savior. Again, the Gnostics believed they were "enlightened" and had completely overcome fleshly tendencies.

Recognizing our sin and our need for a Savior is the first step toward fellowship with God. Ignoring our sin is the greatest deception of all. Here's how John put it:

1 JOHN 1:8-10

If we claim to be without sin, we deceive ourselves and the truth is not in us. If we confess our sins, he is faithful and just and will forgiveus our sins and purify us from all unrighteousness. If we claim we have not sinned, we make him out to be a liar and his word is not in us.

To confess something is much more than just admitting guilt. Confession really means to speak in agreement with someone else. To confess our sins, as John says here, means that we agree with God that we have sinned and need atonement for that sin. Author Warren Wiersbe writes, "Confession simply means being honest with ourselves and with God, and if others are involved, being honest with them too."[15] God's Word is clear—all have sinned, and there is no one righteous—no, not one. If we claim we have not sinned, we make God out to be a liar.

Most of us don't want to see our own sin. We would rather hide it than bring it to the light. If we walk in the light, we let God shine His light into our lives. We are honest about our sin and agree with Him that we have sinned. If we walk in the darkness, we deceive ourselves and think that we haven't sinned, or at least haven't sinned badly enough to need a Savior. For those who agree with God that they are sinners, God is faithful and just. He forgives us our sins and purifies us from all (there's that word again) unrighteousness.

Some people mistakenly think this verse means that we need to make sure we confess every sin, and if we miss one we may not be saved. But if we take this verse in light of Scripture as a whole, we understand that salvation comes through faith in Christ. John reminds us that it is the blood of Christ that purifies us from all sin, not our confession. Yet confession is important in our relationship to our heavenly Father. Just as a child may come and confess something to the parent in order to get it off his chest and renew the relationship, so we come to God and confess our sins. We walk in the light as He reveals our sin, and we confess it and maintain that beautiful fellowship with Him.

Through faith in Christ we have become God's children, and He sees us through the blood of His Son. Our confessing specific sins relieves our feelings of distance from the Father when we know we have done something that displeases Him. Because of what Christ did on the cross, God is both faithful and just to forgive us. Think about these two descriptions of God. He is faithful, and we can depend on His faithfulness to forgive us of our sins through Christ. He is just, and because He is just, He cannot allow sinful man into His holy presence, so we must depend on Christ's blood to purify us.

Our Advocate

It's usually not a good thing when you hear the words, "You'd better get a lawyer." Typically that means you are in some sort of trouble. The word *advocate* refers to a lawyer. The basic meaning of the word is one who stands beside you in your defense (Greek, *parakletos*). It's beautiful to realize we have an advocate, one who stands with us in our defense. John didn't want anyone to sin, but he also knew that we all do sin at times, so he gave this word of encouragement.

1 JOHN 2:1-2

My dear children, I write this to you so that you will not sin. But if anybody does sin, we have an advocate with the Father—Jesus Christ, the Righteous One. He is the atoning sacrifice for our sins, and not only for ours but also for the sins of the whole world.

We are not left alone to plead our own case. The Lord God has appointed the perfect lawyer for us. He is Christ, the one and only one who is righteous. He is the only one who can plead our case—Jesus the Righteous One, who knew no sin. This passage paints a glorious picture of what God has done for us by sending His perfect Son as our advocate. In a broader scope the term *advocate* means a comforter, consoler, one who is called to our side to help. Interestingly, Jesus used the same term to describe the Holy Spirit, who is the Helper (Comforter, Advocate) for Christ's followers.

Jesus was the atoning sacrifice for our sins. An atoning sacrifice is one that appeases or satisfies the condition between two parties. In our case it appeases holy God in His relationship with sinful man. John MacArthur wrote about this verse, saying, "The sacrifice of Jesus on the cross satisfied the demands of God's holiness for the punishment of sin."[6] As believers in Christ, we can live in thankfulness for what Christ did on the cross, having once and for all paid the debt for our sins. It is not what we do for God that atones for our sins; it is what He did for us on the cross. What Christ did for us on the cross was sufficient to pay for the sins of all who believe.

Do you see the beautiful picture this paints? Christ standing by our side before the Father, as our advocate, is the one who paid the price for our sin. We are forgiven—we are purified because of what He has done. Take a moment to dwell on His love and goodness toward you. You are not alone—you have an Advocate, One who stands by your side. He is your Comforter, and He is the One who gave His life for you. Be still right now—close your eyes and thank Him for this truth. Feel the warmth of His love lighting up the darkness that creeps into your life in the form of thoughts of your unworthiness before God. You have an Advocate.

Live As Jesus Did

Imagine if you and I met on the street, and I shared with you that I was serving in active duty in the army. You say, "Really—well, where is your uniform?" And I answer, "Oh, that camouflage material just doesn't look good on me, so I've decided to wear this cute pink outfit instead."

Hmm, you start thinking. "Well, what did your officers say about that when you went to boot camp?" I answer, "Oh, I didn't want to get all hot and sweaty at boot camp, so I just didn't show up. I know what to do anyway. I didn't need that basic training stuff."

Scratching your head, you ask, "Well, don't they have rules about showing up for boot camp and stuff?" I respond with, "I don't know, I didn't really pay attention. All those rules are such a bore. I'm just glad to be a part of the military. I hope to be an officer myself one day. It sure is fun to be a part of the group."

At this point you must conclude that in fact I am *not* enlisted in the army (or not playing with a full deck). People in the army follow the commands. It's part of being in the military. If you don't want to follow the commands, then don't enlist in the military. It's as simple as that. Order is a good thing. If the military is to carry out its mission and purpose, the soldiers must look like and act like they belong in it by following orders. Conforming to the military's code of conduct and commands is what sets the military apart from civilians. If someone claims to be in the military, they must look like it and live like it.

Now why did I mention the military scenario? Just as obeying the military's commands demonstrates that a person is genuinely a part of the military, so following Christ's commands reflects an internal faith in Christ. The apostle John wanted the early Christians to get the idea that outward obedience demonstrates that a person has truly experienced salvation. To be sure, obedience doesn't make us saved, just like following military rules doesn't automatically enlist us. The obedience is simply a reflection of our status. Fortunately, you can't get kicked out of God's family—the military may be a different story.

Some people claim to know God, but choose not to obey His commands. John addresses the disconnect here as he says obedience and living in Christ go hand in hand. You will begin to see that John restates in different ways certain particular themes throughout this letter. One of those themes is the fact that if we say we walk with God, there should be evidence of it in how we live. Our lives ought to reflect our relationship with Him.

Here's what John wrote:

1 JOHN 2:3-6

We know that we have come to know him if we keep his commands. Whoever says, "I know him," but does not do what he commands is a liar, and the truth is not in that person. But if anyone obeys his word, love for God is truly made complete in them. This is how we know we are in him: Whoever claims to live in him must live as Jesus did.

Bottom line, if we claim to follow Jesus, then we must live as He lived. So how did He live? He lived a life of bold, pure love. In fact, He exemplified love in every way. He reached out and touched the diseased and the sinners and the poor. He loved the children. He loved the outcasts. He loved the ones who didn't look so pretty on the outside. He wasn't impressed by social status of the scribes and Pharisees, who appeared outwardly perfect; He cared about people's hearts. Jesus submitted His will to the Father's will. Jesus served others, though He Himself deserved to be served. Jesus humbled Himself by coming in the flesh as a man and laying down His life for us. He loved and forgave even His enemies. He walked in obedience to the Father.

Jesus showed us what true love looks like. Perhaps you are thinking, *But I will never be able to demonstrate that kind of bold and pure love. I can't even make it through the day without yelling at my kids or grumbling at my co-worker.* So your love isn't perfect? Only God's love is, but the beautiful thing is that we can go to our Father and ask Him to help us love. He can boldly and purely love through us.

We are not alone. As we walk in the light and in fellowship with Him, we can ask the God of love to help us love like He does. His very nature is love. Only through Him can we love in the refreshing and powerful way that Jesus loved. Without Christ, we cannot possibly live and love in these extraordinary ways. It is His love in us that is able to change the world around us.

> *Father, I want to live like Jesus did. I want to demonstrate Your love to this dark and hurting world. My love may be weak, but where I am weak You are strong. Love boldly and purely through me. Give me a love that goes beyond status and convenience. Demonstrate Your love through me in my actions and my words. Let the light of Your love shine on the dark places in my heart, so that I might love those whom I thought I couldn't love. Help those around me see what Jesus' love looks like as they see Your love shining brightly through me.*

Getting Personal

ABIDING TRUTHS:

- God is light and in Him is no darkness at all.
- If we claim to have fellowship with God, we must walk in the light as He is in the light.
- Recognize and confess your sin.
- He is the atoning sacrifice for our sins.
- Jesus is our Advocate, the One who stands beside us in our defense.
- Live like Jesus, obeying His commands.
- Seek His help to demonstrate a bold and pure love.

ADDITIONAL READING: John 15

ACTION STEPS: Daily light

Just as the light of the sun illuminates each new day, so the light of God's Word lights our path as we walk along the way. The Bible not only shines the light on the dark corners of our lives, revealing sin and pointing out dangerous paths; it also reminds us of and refreshes us with the truth of God's love for us. Saturate your mind and heart each day with His Word. Set aside a time to read the Bible in the morning, taking in the message of His truth and applying it personally to your life throughout your day.

Allow His Word to shine in some of the dusty corners of your heart, where you may have allowed a pattern of sin to grow. Hidden sins like bitterness, unforgiveness, and anger tend to hide out in our hearts sometimes, not visible to the eye. As God reveals your sin, confess it and ask Him to create a clean heart in you as you move forward.

Make a plan to study God's Word each day. I suggest using a study Bible, which has notes to help increase your understanding. Purchase a journal and write at least one truth God shows you from His Word each day.

I commit to personally pursue God's Word each day:

Place: _____

Time: _____

_____ *Bought journal*

_____ *Began writing on* _____

PART TWO

Doing the Will of God

*"The primary test of life is not service but love,
both for man and for God."*
WILLIAM STILL

*"I urge you, brothers and sisters, in view of God's mercy,
to offer your bodies as a living sacrifice,
holy and pleasing to God—
this is your true and proper worship.
Do not conform to the pattern of this world,
but be transformed by the renewing of your mind.
Then you will be able to test
and approve what God's will is—
his good, pleasing and perfect will."*
ROMANS 12:1-2

CHAPTER THREE

The New and Improved You

"He who is not filled with love is necessarily small,
withered, shriveled in his outlook on life and things."
BENJAMIN B. WARFIELD

"This is my command: Love each other."
JOHN 15:17

I s it possible for a woman to have the love of Christ dwelling within her heart, and yet harbor hatred toward other people? John says the two cannot co-exist. One is light and the other is darkness. What about the cruel and hateful things that have been done throughout the ages in the name of religion and Christianity? What about the local church that split because of the hateful bickering between the members? What about the protesters who hatefully and loudly condemn sinners? What about the middle-school girl who felt like an outcast and was laughed at by the mean girls in her church youth group?

Sadly, people claim the name of Christ when in fact they do not demonstrate or possess the love of Christ at all. There are many who claim to know Him, yet the truth is not evidenced in their life. If you have ever been hurt by a hateful person or a malicious so-called "Christian" then this chapter may bring a new ray of emotional healing and hope to your heart. If you are harboring hatred in your heart or have been hurtful or spiteful toward a brother or sister in Christ, then this chapter may have a sobering message for you as well.

Jesus warned about those who claimed to have a connection with God, but were really living a lie. He said,

> *Watch out for false prophets. They come to you in sheep's clothing, but inwardly they are ferocious wolves. By their fruit you will recognize them. Do people pick grapes from thornbushes, or figs from thistles? Likewise, every good tree bears good fruit, but a bad tree bears bad fruit. A good tree cannot bear bad fruit, and a bad tree cannot bear good fruit. Every tree that does not bear good fruit is cut down and thrown into the fire. Thus, by their fruit you will recognize them.* [1]

When I go to the grocery store, it is fairly easy to figure out which fruit is the bad fruit and which is the good fruit. Take peaches, for instance—the bad ones are brown and squishy. It's not too difficult to set those aside. Every once in a while I'll buy some peaches that look good on the outside, and yet when I get them home and slice them up they are grainy or yucky on the inside. As I have gotten older I have become a little more discerning about my peach purchases. Yes, I'm one of those silly ladies who squeeze and sniff the peaches before buying them. Honestly, I've found if they smell good and are fairly firm, then they are good on the inside too.

Outward appearances can be deceiving. Just because there are baskets of peaches available at the grocery store doesn't mean every peach is a good peach. In a similar way, just because a person goes to church doesn't mean they have the love of Christ dwelling in them. In the book of Galatians, the apostle Paul gave us a "peach test," if you will. First he gave the Galatians a description of the type of actions that demonstrate that Christ's Spirit is *not* in that person. Here's what he wrote:

> *The acts of the flesh are obvious: sexual immorality, impurity and debauchery; idolatry and witchcraft; hatred, discord, jealousy, fits of rage, selfish ambition, dissensions, factions and envy; drunkenness, orgies, and the like. I warn you, as I did before, that those who live like this will not inherit the kingdom of God.* [2]

The reason Paul says these people will not inherit the kingdom of God is not because of their bad behavior, but rather because their behavior demonstrates that God's Spirit is not dwelling in them. Notice terms like *hatred, discord,* and *fits of rage.* That's not typically the deeds of someone who has the love of Christ in them. Actually, these people are not peaches at all. They may look like peaches, but when you examine them carefully, they are false peaches. Probably apricots. Wait a minute—I like apricots. They are probably persimmons, which look kind of like peaches but certainly don't taste like them. (Okay, so I may be taking this peach analogy too far.)

On the other hand, Paul gave a good peach description. Here are the qualities that give evidence to the love of Christ dwelling in a person:

> *The fruit of the Spirit is love, joy, peace, forbearance, kindness, goodness, faithfulness, gentleness and self-control. Against such things there is no law. Those who belong to Christ Jesus have crucified the flesh with its passions and desires. Since we live by the Spirit, let us keep in step with the Spirit.* [3]

Personally, I think that description is peachy! I'd much rather have the fruit that comes as a result of God's Spirit rather than the qualities that develop apart from Him. In this chapter we are going to learn what John has to say about the characteristics of a sincere follower of Christ.

Something New

Generally speaking, I like new things. For instance, I like to try new recipes or visit new restaurants. I like to purchase a new outfit or a new pair of shoes now and then. The Greeks used two different words for "new." One, *neos*, meant new in time, in the same way that we may use the word *recent* ("I recently purchased a new outfit."). The other term, *kainos*, meant new in quality, representing something fresh and updated ("I'm getting rid of all the stuff in my closet and going for a whole new look—a total transformation or extreme makeover."). John wanted the early Christians to know that the command to love each other is not a new or recent command, yet actually Christ gave us a fresh new way of experiencing a transformational love.

John almost sounds confused here. He says that he is "not writing a new command," and then he turns right around and says he is. Sounds a bit confusing, but the command to love is not new. Yet Christ's love is a new kind of love. His love completely changes us, and transforms the way we love others. Ultimately the most important truth that John is trying to portray is that true love is only found in Christ.

Here's what John wrote:

I JOHN 2:7-8

Dear friends, I am not writing you a new command but an old one, which you have had since the beginning. This old command is the message you have heard. Yet I am writing you a new command; its truth is seen in him and in you, because the darkness is passing and the true light is already shining.

This is not the first time John wrote about this new command. In his Gospel he quoted Jesus as saying, "A new command I give you: Love one another. As I have loved you, so you must love one another. By this everyone will know that you are my disciples if you love one another."[4] Again, loving others is not a new command, but without Christ we are not able to truly experience God's love and show it to others. His love is revolutionary. His love was a sacrificial love, not a what's-in-it-for-me kind of love.

We see this word *new* (*kainos*) in other places in the New Testament. Paul described believers as a "new [*kainos*] creation." He wrote to the Ephesians that they had been taught to "put on your new [*kainos*] nature, created to be like God—truly righteous and holy" (4:24 NLT). Yes, there is a difference, a newness, that Christ's love brings to our lives.

Recently I was handed a pamphlet written by one of my former fellow teachers at Trinity Christian Academy in Dallas. Jim Eckhardt was an insightful Bible teacher there at TCA and impacted many lives in a positive way. Years ago he wrote a devotional, which was reprinted and handed out at his funeral. Jim found joy in the transforming newness Christ brought to his life. Here's a practical and powerful thought he shared:

> I tried for years to live the Christian life as a "forgiven sinner." And I failed miserably. How can a sinner, even a forgiven sinner, ever hope to live a holy life? Only a saint (one who is holy) can live a holy life!
>
> Now don't get me wrong. I'm not saying I am sinless. But neither am I the same person I was before I was saved. When I trusted Christ as my Saviour, He did much more than simply forgive my sins, wonderful as that is. He made me, in my deepest personhood, a new person, a holy person. Now that I realize this, I can better understand: "If anyone is in Christ, he is a new [*kainos*] creation; the old has gone, the new has come!"
>
> Christians are radically different people! (The term *radical* comes from the Latin word for *root* and means "the essential core or the heart.") At the very center of my being I am a new person. I am radically different from the person I was before I was born again. I am radically different from non-Christians.[5]

The newness we have in Christ enables us to live and love in a richer and deeper way. We are no longer slaves to sin; we are no longer walking in darkness. Instead we are God's children, radically different, new, fresh, changed from the inside out. He gives us the capacity to love and forgive in a new and broader sense. Not by our own power. We have the power of the living God dwelling in us in the form of His Spirit. As we continue through John's epistle, take note of the numerous times he refers to having God's Spirit in us. Remember, we walk in fellowship (partnership)—we do not live and love on our own.

Jesus gave us a new and refreshing way to love. A Jesus-type love is patient and kind. It doesn't envy or boast, it is not proud or rude. It keeps no record of wrongs. His love does not delight in evil, but rejoices with the truth. It always protects, always hopes, always trusts, always perseveres. His love never fails. Christ's love is uniting between believers and inviting to those who don't know Him. Those who hate others are still in spiritual darkness. Those who love like Jesus shine brightly, lighting up a dark world with God's truth.

In his epistle, John often wrote in terms of contrasts and absolutes: light/darkness, life/death, love/hate, truth/lie. Here we see he continues the analogy between the contrasts of love/hate and light/dark:

1 JOHN 2:9-11

Anyone who claims to be in the light but hates a brother or sister is still in the darkness. Anyone who loves their brother and sister lives in the light, and there is nothing in them to make them stumble. But anyone who hates a brother or sister is in the darkness and walks around in the darkness. They do not know where they are going, because the darkness has blinded them.

Recently my husband, Curt, and I attended a dinner party where we sat at a table with a nationally renowned optic surgeon. He shared with us several amazing stories about saving people from living a life of blindness. Statistics show that, of their five senses, people most dread losing their sense of sight. Although people dread the thought of not being able to see, how much worse is it to be blinded by the darkness of our own hatred. If we hate our brother or sister in Christ, then we are blinded spiritually. We walk around in the darkness, stumbling and possibly hurting others in our path.

Often it's easy to recognize hateful and cruel actions of others, but it's not so easy to detect the hidden hatred that dwells within our own hearts. We must open our eyes to the not-so-obvious hatred that lurks within. Yes, there in the dark regions of our own heart we must ask the Lord to shine His light and convict us personally of hatred, bitterness, and unforgiveness that we have allowed to grow and develop. If we say we have no sin we deceive ourselves. Let us ask God to open our eyes so we can see and get rid of the ugly and dark hatred which tends to blind us. As David wrote,

> *The commands of the Lord are radiant,*
> *giving light to the eyes...*
>
> *Who can discern their own errors?*
> *Forgive my hidden faults.*
> *Keep your servant also from willful sins;*
> *may they not rule over me.*
> *Then I will be blameless,*
> *innocent of great transgression.*
>
> *May these words of my mouth and this meditation of my heart*
> *be pleasing in your sight,*
> *Lord, my Rock and my Redeemer.*[6]

The light of His love dispels the darkness and in its place brings warmth, strength, and security. The darkness of hatred and the ugliness of bitterness only bring danger, loss, hurt, fear, and separation. I want to walk in the light as Jesus is in the light. I want to see where I am going and light the path for others. Don't you want to do the same?

> *Father, just as Your love is a light in our lives, so*
> *let us be lights shining brightly for You. Let our*
> *Christlike love light up the area around us, so that*
> *others may see our good works and glorify You.*

Reasons for Writing

As an author, I am often asked to do radio interviews about my books. I love it. From my own home I can speak to people all over the country, encouraging them and sharing the truth of God's love. Now can you guess what the most frequently asked question is to any author during an interview? If you guessed, *Why did you write this book?* you're right. That's the one question I'm continually asked, and I'd better have a pretty compelling answer to go along with it. Most of the time, an author's motivation and who he or she is writing to helps potential readers make a connection with the author. If I simply say, "I don't know, I just wanted to write it," then I haven't endeared myself to anyone. But if I respond by sharing that I had a desire in my own life to embrace God's love and deepen my understanding of it and I want other women to know His love too, then you may be more interested in knowing what I have to say.

John was kind enough to give us a good answer to the question, "Why did you write this book and who is it for?" Here in the middle of his letter, he lets us in on his motivation and his audience. Earlier in the letter he told us that he wrote these things to make his joy complete. But now we see that his joy will be complete as he sees his fellow believers stay strong in their faith:

1 JOHN 2:12-14

I am writing to you, dear children,
    because your sins have been forgiven on account of his name.
I am writing to you, fathers,
    because you know him who is from the beginning.
I am writing to you, young men,
    because you have overcome the evil one.

I write to you, dear children,
    because you know the Father.
I write to you, fathers,
    because you know him who is from the beginning.

I write to you, young men,
  because you are strong,
  and the word of God lives in you,
  and you have overcome the evil one.

Children? Fathers? Young men? What did John mean by these titles? All of the titles represent members of a family, and isn't that what we are in the body of Christ? How lovely of John to use these rich terms. Perhaps you noticed the repetition of certain phrases. John addresses children twice, but in the first verse the word for children is *teknia* (singular, *teknion),* implying general offspring of any age. It was a kindly address often used by teachers toward their students or disciples in a way of tender appeal. We see John's use of it often throughout his letters as he addressed believers and warned them of spiritual dangers.

I love how he identified the children of God, as ones whose "sins have been forgiven on account of his name." Oh what a glorious truth as believers in Christ! We are a part of His family because of what Jesus did on the cross. God no longer sees our sin. He sees Christ's righteousness instead. Our sins are forgiven on account of His name! Great joy fills my heart when I consider this one phrase. It is not what we have done that has pardoned us, but rather what He has done. It is all because of Him.

> *We thank You, Lord Jesus, for our sins are forgiven*
> *on account of Your wonderful name.*

When we see the word *children* a second time in the passage ("I write to you, dear children, because you know the Father") it is actually a different word, *paidia* (singular, *paidion),* referring to infants or young children. John is most likely referring here to the youngest believers in the family of God. This is the same word Jesus used when He instructed the disciples to "let the little children come to me, and do not hinder them, for the kingdom of God belongs to such as these."[7] How important it is to instruct the little ones! We must be continually aware of the young hearts and minds ready to absorb the truth of God's Word. Do not neglect to teach the little ones and help develop their faith in Christ. Jesus valued the children, and we ought to do the same.

We see in our passage that John used the word *fathers* twice. Fathers were most likely those who were mature in their faith, ones who had known Christ for a while and were now leaders in the body of believers. You could think of them as elders, respected ones in the faith. John addresses the fathers as the ones who have known Christ from the beginning (the beginning of Christianity and perhaps were even eyewitnesses of Jesus). Yet although they were fathers, they still needed continued instruction concerning the faith. And don't we all? We are never too old or mature to grow in our understanding of our faith. We should be learners until the day Christ takes us home.

The final group John addressed was the "young men." He described the young men as having overcome the evil one, being strong, and having the Word of God living in them. The Word of God and overcoming temptation go hand in hand. David wrote, "How can a young person stay on the path of purity? By living according to your word...I have hidden your word in my heart that I might not sin against you."[8] Does the Word of God live in you? Do you feed on it daily, meditate on it, and allow it to permeate your very being? Memorizing God's Word helps us to stay strong and overcome the evil one.

The young and strong people are vital in the body of believers. I think about the young women God uses to passionately teach His Word in today's culture. He continually raises up strong and vibrant young warriors to teach, train, and live out His Word effectively in the world. Just as Paul charged Timothy to not let anyone despise him because of his youth, so young men and women of the faith who are rooted and founded in God's Word should be encouraged to continue in the work for the Lord, proclaiming His message of truth and love.

John Calvin wrote his opinion about why John so wisely addressed the various groups who would read this letter:

> A general address produces less effect; we are so perverse
> that few of us think that what is addressed to everyone

belongs to us. Old people mostly excuse themselves because they are past the age of learning; children refuse to learn, saying they are not yet old enough; the middle-aged do not pay attention because they are occupied with other things. So then, lest anyone should exempt themselves, the apostle mentions three ages, the most common divisions of human life.[9]

There you have it—this letter is personal. It's for each one of us no matter where we are on our faith journey or how old we are in our life journey. How many times have you heard a sermon and thought, *I wish so-and-so was here to hear this message*? John is saying the message from this letter is for everyone.

The Rest of the Story

Now we know who John was writing to, but what was his true motivation? What really compelled him to write this letter to the early believers? Early Christian tradition reveals that a teacher named Cerinthus was a contemporary and an opponent of the apostle. Although Cerinthus followed some claims of Christianity, he denied that the Supreme God had made the physical world, and he denied the divinity of Jesus. He believed that "the Christ" had come to Jesus at baptism and guided Him through ministry, but had then left Him at the crucifixion. Cerinthus was considered one of the early Gnostics.

John was so concerned about Cerinthus's influence on the early Christians that it is believed that he wrote his Gospel as well as his first and second epistles to warn against such heresy and establish a firm understanding of Christian doctrine. The story is told by Polycarp (one of the early Church Fathers, who lived from about AD 69–155 and was a disciple of John's) of a particular incident where John fled from a bathhouse when he found out that Cerinthus was inside. As he ran, John shouted, "Let us flee, lest the building fall down; for Cerinthus, the enemy of the truth, is inside!"[10] John's zeal for the truth not only led him to flee the bathhouse but to make sure the truth was written far and wide for all to know.

Pastor Greg Metcalf describes the ultimate advantage this had for you and me:

> The benefit and blessing of Cerinthus to the church was that it caused the early church to wrestle with and define the character and nature of Jesus Christ. It also resulted in John the Apostle defining the character of God as involved in the redemption of sinners. What a wonderful scheme of God to allow a heretic such as Cerinthus to rise up and challenge the teachings of Jesus in order to inspire John to write an epistle that clearly delineated God's plan of redemption.[11]

What a positive way to look at an "enemy of the truth." Never underestimate what God can do through the adversity you face. He has a bigger and better plan. There are many Cerinthus-type people in our culture today, who take the truth and twist it or proclaim half-truths mixed with their own philosophies. Do not be deceived and do not be discouraged. Know the truth, hold on to it, and proclaim it lovingly and boldly.

Getting Personal

ABIDING TRUTHS:

- God's command is clear—love one another.
- Jesus gave us a fresh picture of love.
- If we claim to live in Him we must live like Jesus did, loving with a bold, pure love.
- Just as darkness and light cannot co-exist, neither can the love of Christ co-exist with hatred for our brothers and sisters in Christ.
- John's message speaks to each of us no matter where we are at or what age we are.

- Take notice of the children and teach them in the ways of the Lord.

ADDITIONAL READING: 1 Corinthians 13

ACTION STEPS: Harboring hatred?

Take some time to be still before the Lord and ask Him to reveal any hatred toward a brother or sister in Christ that may be lurking in your heart. Ask Him to bring to mind any past hurts or festering bitterness that you may be un-wittingly holding on to. Seek the Lord's conviction if you have maligned or gossiped or told half-true stories about people. Allow God to shine His light, and ask for His forgiveness. Ask also for His help as you move forward and move away from hatred, and instead grow rich and full in love. Take time to thank God for His unfailing love and forgiveness toward you. Rejoice in the love He has for His own, then reflect His love to a hurting world.

Write out your own prayer of thankfulness to God for His love, forgiveness, and help._____

_____

_____

_____

_____

_____

_____

Chapter Four

*W*ho Do You Love?

*"All that man can know of God
and his love in this life
is revealed in Jesus Christ."*

A.W. Tozer

*"Jesus replied: 'Love the Lord your God with all your heart
and with all your soul and with all your mind.
This is the first and greatest commandment.'"*

Matthew 22:37-38

Trisha enjoys driving the luxury car her husband bought her on her fortieth birthday. She appreciates it, but would be just as happy in an old pickup truck. Honestly, she sometimes wishes she had one when she goes downtown to serve the homeless. Trisha's home is elaborate and expansive, yet she is thankful for a nice place where she can open up the doors for ministry meetings and banquets and provide a room for an occasional visiting pastor or missionary. She wears beautiful clothes, some of the latest fashions, which she buys from resale shops and discount stores. She never pays full price for anything, and always gives away clothes from her closet before bringing in new ones.

If you were to simply see Trisha and size her up according to what she owns or what she looks like on the outside, you might assume she is enamored by this world and all the glitz and glamour it offers. But looks can be deceiving. Trisha appreciates what she has, but she holds her material possessions with open hands and recognizes that each of them can be used for a purpose. She doesn't love the things—she loves the Creator of all things. She lives with honest and simple contentment where she is at, not trying to be something she is not. Love and compassion for others are always at the forefront of her mind. She may look rich on the outside, but her true wealth comes from a heart that loves God and serves others.

On the other hand, Rhonda drives a compact car, and all appearances indicate that she is not attached to the things of this world. She dresses modestly, and one would assume that her quiet and demure mood reflect a loving spirit. Yet her heart reveals a different story. She arrives at church each Sunday filled with anger and resentment as she compares herself to other women. During the worship service she convenes a mental court, sitting in judgment and condemning all the people who selfishly spend money on themselves. Jealousy festers in her thoughts as she thinks about all the things she could have had if her life or job or marriage had turned out differently.

Rhonda spends a good amount of her time each day gossiping about those who have it "easy." She feels as though it is her right to malign others since she has been given such a bad lot in life. She feels no remorse over her hatred and bitterness, and actually seems to revel in it. Gratitude toward God and serving others have no place in her life. When she is not busy complaining, she loves, loves, loves to shop at estate sales and garage sales. It's her passion and consumes many hours every week.

Two profiles of two women who love and live very differently. The stories serve as a reminder that it is the heart, not the outward stuff, that truly matters. We must be careful about judging outward appearances when it comes to worldliness. Assumptions are easy to make, but only

God sees the heart. Now I don't want you to use these stories as a motivation to try to judge other people's hearts. I've told you these stories so we each may examine our own heart and consider the love for the world that tends to abide there. God cares about what we love. He calls us to love Him and love others. He tells us not to love this world. John wrote,

1 JOHN 2:15-17

Do not love the world or anything in the world. If anyone loves the world, love for the Father is not in them. For everything in the world—the lust of the flesh, the lust of the eyes, and the pride of life—comes not from the Father but from the world. The world and its desires pass away, but whoever does the will of God lives forever.

In theological circles, some groups tend to camp on certain issues about possessions. Recently we have seen a rise of both the prosperity theology (God wants you to be rich) and the poverty theology (God wants you to be poor). We must be cautious of both. If we take Scripture as a whole, we see God placed some people in positions of wealth (Abraham, David, Solomon, Nicodemus, Lydia), and others in a place of poverty with very few possessions (Jesus, John the Baptist, many of the disciples). It's not about the money or the possessions. It's about what is central to our heart! We have a choice as to where we will place our affections. So we must ask ourselves, "What do I worship? Is it Christ or is it creation?"

Pastor John Henry Jowett said this: "Worldliness is a spirit, a temperament, an attitude of soul. It is life without high callings, life devoid of lofty ideals. It is a gaze horizontal, never vertical. Its motto is 'Forward,' never 'Upward.'"[1] When our heart, our gaze, is on the Lord, it leaves very little room for worldliness. But when our heart and mind are wrapped up in what we do or don't have, our affection and love for this world tend to increase. Ralph Venning put it in strong terms: "If men do not put the love of the world to death, the love of the world will put them to death."[2]

John warned believers to guard their hearts against an adoration of or affection toward the things of this world when he wrote, "Do not love the world or anything in the world." What did John mean by "the world"? Throughout the New Testament we see this word, *kosmos,* which generally signifies the earth in contrast to heaven, the sum of temporal possessions, or the present condition of human affairs. In other words, anything connected with this present life and in the ordered universe can be encompassed in the word *world.* Our citizenship is in heaven, and our hearts and affections ought to be pointed toward that kingdom, not this one.

Paul wrote to the Colossians, saying,

> *Since...you have been raised with Christ, set your hearts on things above, where Christ is, seated at the right hand of God. Set your minds on things above, not on earthly things. For you died, and your life is now hidden with Christ in God.*[3]

When I read this verse I'm reminded of how very rich we are in Christ. Paul also told the Colossians,

> *My goal is that they may be encouraged in heart and united in love, so that they may have the full riches of complete understanding, in order that they may know the mystery of God, namely, Christ, in whom are hidden all the treasures of wisdom and knowledge.*[4]

We have riches this world does not recognize. We who are in Christ are wealthy indeed! We are daughters of the King of kings, and our heart's desire ought to be toward Him. John wrote in his Gospel that, to all who believed Christ and accepted Him He gave the right to become children of God. We have been raised out of our spiritual poverty or captivity and brought into the royal family. Our true wealth is found in knowing we are loved and forgiven by God and that we are a part of His kingdom.

If we use a fairy-tale analogy, just as Rapunzel's life changed from the moment she met her prince, so our life changes when we meet Christ. We have a new life in Christ, and we are citizens of His kingdom! Now imagine if Rapunzel had this new life awaiting her in the kingdom, but she still craved her old life and old way of doing things in the dark and terrible tower. She would continue to be a slave to the old way of living instead of being free to live in the joy that the kingdom and the handsome prince offered. It's amazing how easily the desires in this world can distract us "princesses" and cause us to steer our love away from our Prince and His kingdom.

The difference between the prince's kingdom and evil captivity seems so clear in fairy tales, but often it is not as easily recognized in day-to-day life. The apostle John points out the sharp contrast between the love of this world and the love of God and that you can't love both. He described "everything in the world" using three broad and memorable phrases: *the lust of the flesh, the lust of the eyes,* and *the pride of life.* Hmm…I recognize those types of temptations. Consider the very first sin in the garden—Eve saw the fruit (lust of the eyes) and tasted it (lust of the flesh) thinking it would make her like God, having all the knowledge of good and evil (pride of life).

There is nothing new under the sun. Jesus was tempted by Satan in three areas, yet without sin. Remember? He was tempted to turn the stones into bread (lust of the flesh), tempted to jump off the highest point of the temple (pride), and Satan showed Him the splendor of all the kingdoms of the earth (lust of the eyes). Satan keeps going back to his old bag of tricks, trying to make us fall more in love with this world. His ultimate goal is to destroy us by distracting us from having a rich and meaningful love relationship with our Prince.

Rich Toward God…

Author and theologian Andrew Murray referred to the love of the world this way: "There is nothing the Christian life suffers more from than the subtle and indescribable worldliness that comes from the cares of the possessions of this life."[5] It comes so subtly. We may not even recognize the change that begins to take place in our hearts when temptations casually show up in our lives. Like a ship which drifts slowly off course, our affections can slowly drift toward a love for the world. Ships use navigational systems to stay on course, and we must allow God's Word and His Spirit to guide our hearts and draw us back to a Christ-centered affection. Recently at church we recited the following confession:

> *O Righteous Father, You call me to look upon the beauty and glory of Your Son, but I have turned my gaze to the transient and created splendor of this world. I have secretly cherished visions of earthly wealth, beauty, and power and have sought after them instead of the kingdom, the power, and the glory of Jesus. Forgive the wandering eyes of my heart and enable me by faith to fix my gaze upon the One who alone is worthy of all my focused attention and deepest affection.*[6]

May this be our constant and sincere confession. There is a continual war raging within our hearts, and so we must pursue that which is lasting, in the form of righteousness, godliness, faith, love, endurance, and gentleness. Paul in his letter to Timothy referred to the love of money as the root of all kinds of evil. A love for money takes our eyes off of our loving Provider and places our eyes on what this world can provide. Again, Paul is not speaking against money or possessions in themselves, but against the love of these things.

Jesus also warned about greed by using the illustration of a rich man:

> *"Beware! Guard against every kind of greed. Life is not measured by how much you own." Then he told them a story: "A rich man had a fertile farm that produced fine crops. He said to himself, 'What should I do? I don't have room for all my crops.' Then he said, 'I know! I'll tear down my barns and build bigger ones. Then I'll have room enough to store all my wheat and other goods. And I'll sit back and say to myself, "My friend, you*

have enough stored away for years to come. Now take it easy!
Eat, drink, and be merry!"' But God said to him, 'You fool!
You will die this very night. Then who will get everything you
worked for?' Yes, a person is a fool to store up earthly wealth
but not have a rich relationship with God."[7]

Whether you have many possessions or live very simply, whether you have loads of money in the bank or just enough to get by, the question is the same: "Are you rich toward God?" Every single one of us has the opportunity to be wealthy in God's kingdom by laying up treasures in heaven. A woman who loves God with her whole being and loves others with sincerity and compassion is a wealthy woman. A woman who allows herself to be consumed by what she doesn't have or who is constantly wanting more is falling into that dangerous trap of love for the world. When we crave the things of this world to satisfy our desires physically and emotionally, we will only end up bankrupt, spiritually speaking.

What do those cravings look like in a practical sense in today's world? Let's take a deeper look at the three terms John used in his letter: *the lust of the flesh, the lust of the eyes,* and *the pride of life.* The lust of the flesh refers to cravings and desires we have physically. Satan uses the struggles of overeating, undereating, drugs, alcohol, sex, and the like to distract people from the love of God. It's easy to think of indulging in the flesh as the naughty sins that other people do, but it may even be the simple things that draw us away from trusting the goodness of God to satisfy our desires.

John Calvin wrote about physical desires and cravings:

> When a corrupt lust of this kind rules in us and so holds us entangled that we do not think about the heavenly life, we are possessed by an animal stupidity…a life in which people become so degenerate that they are satisfied with the present life and think no more of immortal life than mute animals. So then, whoever makes himself a slave to earthly lusts in this way cannot be of God.[8]

Now I like my dogs, but honestly, Calvin is right, when we get tangled up in just having our needs met and allow our love for God to grow cold, we are quite similar to my big giant mastiffs, who simply live to eat and sleep and go on an occasional walk. God intended for our lives to be much more rich and meaningful than those of dogs. He gave each of us a soul that desires satisfaction beyond the physical. Some people spend their lives chasing after one craving or another, trying to satisfy their physical needs when it is really their soul that is hungry. Let us not starve our soul from the love of God because we are so distracted by our physical desires.

How is the lust of the eyes different than the lust of the flesh? The lust of the eyes represents the wanting and desire for more. The opposite of the lust of the eyes would be contentment. Are we able to be satisfied and content in the place where we are, knowing that our God will supply our needs? Billions of dollars are spent each year on advertising with the basic goal to make us unsatisfied with ourselves and our lives, thinking we need more or better stuff. Every checkout line at the grocery store is filled with magazines trying to make us feel as though we need to look better, feel better, and do better. Now I'm not against improvement and looking for ways to grow and change for the better—I'm just pointing out that it is difficult to escape the desire for more, more, more!

Shelly always looked with envy at the moms who brought their kids to school each day. She wished she could be on the other side of the door dropping her kids off, rather than teaching a room of fifth-graders from eight in the morning until three in the afternoon and then facing homework and dinner with her own family. From her point of view, all those other families had perfect lives. She was jealous of their lifestyle and dreamed night and day about living the life of luxury, but of course that would never happen on her husband's salary. A pastor's income certainly didn't provide enough to buy the cute clothes she wanted.

As Shelly spent time on the Internet, social groups began to draw more and more of her interests away from family time in the evening. *They're old enough to do their own homework*, she reasoned. Besides, she needed some time to unwind and her husband was always busy studying. On one occasion she decided to look up an old crush from high school. *What could it hurt?* she thought. His pictures were intriguing—he certainly looked successful. Light chatting led to more intimate messages and finally meeting for coffee, and…you know where it went from there.

The eyes are never satisfied. They are always looking for more. Is it even possible to be content in today's world? It is when we turn our eyes upward. David wrote, "Those who look to him for help will be radiant with joy."[9] He is the One who meets our needs. As we set our eyes (our desires) on things above, our eyes are turned from the things that satisfy only temporarily. As we fix our eyes on Jesus, we can run with diligence the race set before us. Ah, but it is so easy to turn our eyes toward the things we see here and now. Just as a runner must concentrate his focus on the finish line, so we must concentrate our focus on our wonderful Savior.

In the Psalms we read,

> *I lift up my eyes to the mountains—*
> *where does my help come from?*
> *My help comes from the* LORD,
> *the Maker of heaven and earth.*
> *He will not let your foot slip—*
> *he who watches over you will not slumber;*
> *indeed, he who watches over Israel*
> *will neither slumber nor sleep.*
> *The* LORD *watches over you—*
> *the* LORD *is your shade at your right hand;*
> *the sun will not harm you by day,*
> *nor the moon by night.*
> *The* LORD *will keep you from all harm—*
> *he will watch over your life;*
> *the* LORD *will watch over your coming and going*
> *both now and forevermore.*[10]

Perhaps the beauty of this passage is not simply that the psalmist's eyes were on the Lord for his help, but that the Lord's eyes are continually on His people. Did you notice how often this psalm talks about the Lord watching over us? As we consider the lust of the eyes, remember the Lord's eyes are on us, and He lovingly provides for our needs. Turn your eyes toward the Beautiful One, the One who satisfies. As you lift your gaze upon Him, "the things of this earth will grow strangely dim in the light of His glory and grace," as the song says.

Finally, John talks about the "pride of life," which can include such attitudes as "Look at me—I have all these wonderful possessions." Or "Look at me and admire how much I accomplish." Or "Look at me, I sold all my belongings and am moving to Africa to feed the poor." Again, it's not what we do or have, it's about our heart. Pride can pop up in some of the most godly and good behaviors. Check your heart. Are you doing whatever you are doing out of a sincere love for God and care for others, or are you doing it to make yourself look good and impress people? Granted, I'm not sure we will ever have 100 percent pure motives, but we can always in humility turn our eyes toward God and say, "Help me and create in me a clean heart."

Pride declares, "Because I am so great, God needs me." Humility says, "Because I have weaknesses, I need the Lord." The ultimate pride is to think that I can earn my salvation. Essentially, a godly and sincere humility means to recognize that I was dead in my sins and could not save myself. It was the work Christ did on the cross that saved me, not what I do. Pride is so very deceptive. It can come in the form of good works and deeds. It can come in the form of wanting to look like a "good Christian." It can come in the form of thinking that God demands I do something to earn my own salvation or a right relationship with Him. The only thing we do is humbly receive the gift He gave us through Jesus' death on the cross. Blessed are the poor in spirit, for theirs is the kingdom of heaven.

Bottom line, if you have material possessions, live with a grateful and generous heart. Be open to how God can use what you have for kingdom purposes. Do not love what you have—simply live contentedly as you love and pursue God with all your heart and as you love and serve others. If you do not have much in the way of material possessions or wealth, remember that you can still live with a grateful and generous heart. Be open to how God can use what you do have (your gifts and talents) for kingdom purposes. Do not crave or desire things you cannot have. Simply live contentedly as you love and pursue God with all your heart and as you love and serve others. (Notice I emphasize the same message for both conditions, because it's not about the stuff, it's about the affection.)

John closed his remarks about the dangers of the love for the world by reminding believers that the world will pass away, but those who do the will of God will live forever. Yes, this world is temporary, and we must keep this at the forefront of our minds daily. When we look at the big picture of life, what really matters is what is eternal (God, His Word, and people's souls). Make wise investments. Don't put all of your affections in what will not last. In his notebook, missionary Jim Elliot wrote, "He is no fool who gives what he cannot keep to gain that which he cannot lose."[11] Let us love Christ and pursue Him with our whole hearts.

Matt Redman, who is a worship leader and song writer, reminds all who seek to worship Christ,

> This world is full of fragile loves—Love that abandons, Love that fades, Love that divorces, Love that is self-seeking. But the unquenchable worshipper is different. From a heart so amazed by the Father and His wonders, burns a Love that will not be extinguished. It survives any situation and lives through any circumstance. It will not allow itself to be quenched, for that would heap insult on the Love it lives in response to.[12]

The Last Hour

We are in the closing act of the Great Drama. We are in the final leg of the Great Race. We are in the last hour of the Great Time Clock for this earth. God has been working out His purposes and plans throughout all generations, beginning with the creation of this earth. Christ's ascension from this earth to heaven marked the beginning of the last hour, and we live in anticipation of the day He will return. Until then we live with eager expectancy and hope as we look forward to a new heaven and a new earth, which John wrote about in the book of Revelation. Therefore, one of the reasons it makes no sense to love this world is because its passing is imminent.

John moved from warning us about loving this world to reminding us that this is the last phase in God's time chart, and we need to be aware of those who may try to lead us astray. He used the term *antichrist* to point out those people who denied Jesus is the Christ. Although we read in Revelation that there will be one main Antichrist, John also warns that there will be many antichrists in this last hour. Certainly we have many antichrists today, ones who may even claim a loose association with Christians, but there is one way to know who is a Christian and who is not.

Simple test: Whoever denies that Jesus is the Christ is an antichrist.

It's tempting to think, *Well, those atheists—they are a type of antichrist because they do not believe in God.* Yet there are many cults, factions, and groups that may seem religious and may claim that they follow Jesus, but they deny that He is the Christ—the One whom God sent to offer His life as an atoning sacrifice for our sins. John's warning is just as important today as it was when he wrote it! He loved the Lord Jesus and couldn't stand to see anyone tarnish the gospel with their own ideas and philosophies of who Jesus is or isn't.

Again, in John's day he was particularly concerned with Cerinthus and his influence on Christians, but there are many Cerinthus-type teachers and religions today. Here's how John warned the early believers:

1 JOHN 2:18-23

Dear children, this is the last hour; and as you have heard that the antichrist is coming, even now many antichrists have come. This is how we know it is the last hour. They went out from us, but they did not really belong to us. For if they had belonged to us, they would have remained with us; but their going showed that none of them belonged to us.

> *But you have an anointing from the Holy One, and all of you know the truth. I do not write to you because you do not know the truth, but because you do know it and because no lie comes from the truth. Who is the liar? It is whoever denies that Jesus is the Christ. Such a person is the antichrist—denying the Father and the Son. No one who denies the Son has the Father; whoever acknowledges the Son has the Father also.*

In this passage, the term John uses, "dear children," refers to those who have been born of Christ, no matter what age. Here we see the beautiful and inseparable relationship between the Father and the Son. If you deny the Son, then you don't have the Father. If you acknowledge the Son, then you have the Father also. It's a package deal sealed by the Holy Spirit.

What we believe about the deity of Christ is a definitive foundation of our faith. Jesus is all God and all man. He was born into this world for a purpose. He is the Christ, the awaited Messiah, the Holy One, the Atoning Sacrifice for our sins. Cerinthus, who was of Jewish heritage, denied Jesus' deity and denied His miraculous conception by the Holy Spirit. Remember, he taught that Jesus became Christ at His baptism and was no longer Christ when He was crucified. There are many forms of this type of belief even today. We must be cautious about man's philosophies and teachings blended with a little bit of truth about Jesus. John used strong words to point out that anyone who diminishes the deity of Christ is in fact an antichrist and a liar.

What do you believe about Jesus? It is important to be certain so that you will not be swayed by the philosophies of the latest bestseller or the whims of a popular television talk-show host. The Bible tells us clearly that Jesus is the Christ, the Son of the Living God. He was also the Son of man, born in human form. Dietrich Bonhoeffer said, "If Jesus Christ is not true God, how could he help us? If he is not true man, how could he help us?" The Lamb of God, who took away our sins, is the perfect mediator between holy God and sinful man.

We read Jesus' words to the Pharisees in the Gospel of John:

"You are from below; I am from above. You belong to this world; I do not. That is why I said that you will die in your sins; for unless you believe that I Am who I claim to be, you will die in your sins."

"Who are you?" they demanded.

Jesus replied, "The one I have always claimed to be. I have much to say about you and much to condemn, but I won't. For I say only what I have heard from the one who sent me, and he is completely truthful."[13]

What about you? Do you believe that He is who He claimed to be—Son of God, Son of Man, Savior to the world? We love Him and not the world because we believe that He is the Christ, the One God sent to bear the penalty of our sin. We are rich because He has made us whole and complete in Him. We need no other!

Getting Personal

ABIDING TRUTHS:

- Love for God and love for the world are opposed to each other.
- The lust of the flesh, the lust of the eyes, and the pride of life distract us from the love of Christ.
- The ultimate pride of life is to think we need to add our works to the cross of Christ.
- We are citizens of heaven; this world is temporary.
- Loving God and loving others has eternal value.
- The one who denies that Jesus is the Christ is an antichrist.
- The one who acknowledges the Son has the Father also.
- Know what you believe.

ADDITIONAL READING: Matthew 6

ACTION STEPS: Worry test

What do you worry about? What consumes your thoughts? Sometimes this can be the greatest test of where our heart is and what we love most. Take some time today to do a little love test via a worry exam.

What are the three things that you worry about the most?

1. _____

2. _____

3. _____

Take these to the Father's loving care and ask Him to help you turn your eyes and heart back on Him in each of these three areas. Trust Him as your Provider and ask Him to help you love Him more than these areas that distract your heart. Seek to fall in love with Him in a deeper and truer way as you depend on Him.

PART THREE

Being Beautiful

*"My worth is what I am worth to God,
and that is a marvelous great deal,
for Christ died for me."*

WILLIAM TEMPLE

*"You are altogether beautiful, my darling;
there is no flaw in you."*

SONG OF SOLOMON 4:7

CHAPTER FIVE

Fulfilling Fellowship

"The Holy Spirit is the great beautifier of souls."
JOHN OWEN

*"Just as you received Christ Jesus as Lord,
continue to live your lives in him."*
COLOSSIANS 2:6

Lilly Walters had one of those sixth-grade teachers a person does not soon forget. His name was Mr. Gomm, and Lilly says she came to understand insights and wisdom for life from the stories and quotes he shared in his class. She recalled memorable quips he always said to the class, such as, "Better an hour too early than a minute too late!" One day Mr. Gomm read a poem to the class called "The Touch of the Master's Hand." Anything about hands caught Lilly's attention because she had been in an accident a few months before and lost most of her left hand. The message of this particular poem stayed in her heart.

This is the poem that Mr. Gomm read to the class and that touched Lilly's heart so many years ago:

The Touch of the Master's Hand

It was battered and scarred,
And the auctioneer thought it
Hardly worth his while
To waste his time on the old violin,
But he held it up with a smile.

"What am I bid, good people," he cried,
"Who starts the bidding for me?"
"One dollar, one dollar, do I hear two?"
"Two dollars, who makes it three?"
"Three dollars once, three dollars twice, going for three,"

But, no,
From the room far back a gray-bearded man
Came forward and picked up the bow,
Then wiping the dust from the old violin
And tightening up the strings,
He played a melody, pure and sweet,
As sweet as the angel sings.

The music ceased and the auctioneer
With a voice that was quiet and low,
Said, "What now am I bid for this old violin?"
As he held it aloft with its bow.

"One thousand, one thousand, do I hear two?"
"Two thousand, who makes it three?"
"Three thousand once, three thousand twice,
Going and gone," said he.

The audience cheered,
But some of them cried,
"We just don't understand.
What changed its worth?"

Swift came the reply:
"The Touch of the Master's Hand."

And many a man with life out of tune
All battered with bourbon and gin
Is auctioned cheap to a thoughtless crowd
Much like that old violin.

A mess of pottage, a glass of wine,
A game and he travels on.
He is going once, he is going twice,
He is going and almost gone.

But the Master comes,
And the foolish crowd never can quite understand,
The worth of a soul and the change that is wrought
By the Touch of the Master's Hand.[1]

Thirty years after first hearing that poem, Lilly was creating a typing manual for children who had the use of only one hand, and quite by accident she came across the beloved poem again. She wondered who the author was. When she discovered the author's seldom-told story, it occurred to her that there are few "accidents" in life—not to her hand, nor in this poem coming into her life again at just the perfect time. Imagine her surprise when she found out that the author, Myra Brooks Welch, had lived only a few miles away from her own home in Claremont, California. More surprising for Lilly was to discover that Myra had had her own challenge with her hands.

Lilly recorded some of the information she discovered about Myra. In the following passage she shares some of her insight about the author and how she came to write this beautiful poem:

> Myra Brooks Welch, a resident of La Verne, California, was called "the poet with the singing soul." Hers was a very musical family. As a young woman, Myra's special love was playing the organ. In 1921, she heard a speaker address a group of students. She said she became filled with light, and "Touch of the Master's Hand wrote itself in 30

minutes!" She sent it anonymously to her church news bulletin. She felt it was a gift from God, and didn't need her name on it. Its popularity spread like magic. Finally, several years later, the poem was read at a religious international convention—"author unknown." A young man stood up and said, "I know the author, and it's time the world did too. It was written by my mother, Myra Welch."

Then her name, as well as her other beautiful works of poetry, became known worldwide. All of her poetry told of the rejoicing she had in God's love. What the world did not see was the woman who created these masterpieces: Myra in her wheelchair, battered and scarred from severe arthritis, which had taken away her ability to make music. Instead, her musical soul spoke through her poetry. She took one pencil in each of her badly disabled hands. Using the eraser end, she would slowly type the words, the joy of them outweighing the pain of her efforts. Her words, a joyous expression of the wonders of life, as seen by a singing soul, touched by the Master's Hand.[2]

Transforming Beauty

Oh, the beauty of a life that is changed and transformed by the touch of the Master's love! Scripture reminds us that we were created by God and for God. He is the One who designed us and who gives our life meaning and purpose. He is our life. We can choose to engage with Him and walk closely with Him, or we can choose to try to live apart from Him and try to make music on our own. Jesus reminded the disciples that as we abide in Him and He in us, we will bear much fruit, but without Him we can do nothing. Sounds like the violin, doesn't it? The Master's touch makes the difference.

Do you look to His hands to play His music through you? What delightful melodies are made through our lives when we invite His Spirit to work through us! In the last chapter we read John's words: "You have an anointing from the Holy One, and all of you know the truth." As believers in Christ we have the Holy Spirit dwelling within us. This particular word, *anointing*, was originally translated *unction* in the King James Version. When John told believers that they had an anointing (an unction or an endowment) from the Holy One, he was indicating that they themselves have been made holy, set apart to God. This anointing by the Holy One gives us knowledge and insight that the world does not understand.

C.H. Spurgeon wrote on this very topic,

> Every believer understands that to know God is the highest and best form of knowledge; and this spiritual knowledge is a source of strength to the Christian. It strengthens his faith. Believers are constantly spoken of in the Scriptures as being people who are enlightened and taught by the Lord; they are said to "have an unction from the Holy One," and it is the Spirit's particular office to lead them into all truth, and all this for the increase and the fostering of their faith. [3]

He went on to relate this knowledge to our love for Christ:

> Knowledge strengthens love, as well as faith. Knowledge opens the door, and then through that door we see our Savior. Or, to use another similitude, knowledge paints the portrait of Jesus, and when we see that portrait then we love him. We cannot love a Christ whom we do not know, at least, in some degree. If we know very little about the excellencies of Jesus, what he has done for us, and what he is doing now, we cannot love him much; but the more we know him, the more we shall love him. [4]

The anointing we have from God, the presence of God's Spirit in our lives, teaches us about God. His Spirit allows us to understand God's Word and enriches our knowledge of the Savior and, more important, our love for Him. Yes, the more the Spirit teaches us, the more we know Him, and the more we know Him the more we love Him. How marvelous the work of God is in our lives as His Spirit lives in us, directs us, and teaches us. His light shines through us to bring light to this world. Jesus is the one true Light, yet He also told His followers that we are light: "You are the light of the world. A town built on a hill cannot be hidden. Neither do people light a lamp and put it under a bowl. Instead they put it on its stand, and it gives light to everyone in the house. In the same way, let your light shine before others, that they may see your good deeds and glorify your Father in heaven."[5]

English poet Christina Rossetti beautifully penned these lines:

> Tune me, O Lord, into one harmony
> With Thee, on full responsive vibrant chord;
> Unto Thy praise, all love and melody,
> Tune me, O Lord.

Without the Master's touch our lives are dark and meaningless—without the knowledge of His love. But as His Spirit enlightens our lives, our light shines brightly as we point to Him. When we walk hand in hand with Him in fellowship and in the light of His love, our lives beautifully reflect His character and point to Him. Because His Spirit resides in us, we have the ability to bring light in the form of knowledge, wisdom, and love to this world. Just like the violin in the master's hands, our lives play a new song because of Him. We shine brilliantly with His light so that others see and learn about the Master's love. May God's Spirit be so evident in our lives that we light up dark places with His grace and truth!

> *Father, thank You that we have been given an anointing from You. Thank You that You are present in every believer's life. Thank You for Your truth and love that transform us and make us light in this dark world. Shine brightly through us, Lord Jesus.*

Remaining in the Gospel

A popular book and movie called *The Help* brings to light the sad reality of segregation in the South in the early 1960s. The story exposes many of the arrogant and inhumane prejudices that were deeply imbedded in the culture. Amid the sobering tales of the women who served as "the help" in the book, there is also an element of comic relief. One key ingredient in the story line centers around a chocolate pie made by Minnie. As one of "the help," Minnie finally was fed up with one of the self-centered, egotistical "white ladies," named Hilly, and so she put her words into action. Well, actually she put words into her famous chocolate pie.

Let's just say that Minnie added some rather stinky ingredients to her chocolate pie and then dumped in a ton of vanilla and sugar to cover up for the bad stuff. Hilly ate two pieces of Minnie's famous chocolate pie before she realized something was amiss.

It's amazing how something so awful can be disguised in something that seems so delightful. We can be fooled by food, but we can also be fooled by religions or spiritual concepts or people who say they know the truth. The Gnostics claimed to be enlightened by special knowledge that only a select few could possess.

False teachers abound. What they say may sound good and look pretty. They may even mention Jesus now and then, but they promote philosophies that do not align with Scripture. It is important that we remain in the truth so we can recognize when someone adds faulty and misleading ingredients. We must always go back to the basic truth about the gospel and not move from it. The gospel is clear and unchanging. There are those who try to add to it, distract from it, or work to undermine it through their books, their rules, their regulations, and their false religions. John wanted all believers to be aware of those who want to move us from the sure foundation of the gospel. Denominational differences may come and go, but the core of the gospel is clear. John warned,

1 JOHN 2:24-25

See that what you have heard from the beginning remains in you. If it does, you also will remain in the Son and in the Father. And this is what he promised us—eternal life.

When John talks about "what you have heard from the beginning" he is referring to the time when they first heard the truth about Jesus, the gospel message. What they heard and trusted from the beginning of their Christian walk was the basic truth that Jesus Christ is God's Son who came to this world in the flesh and offered His life as an atoning sacrifice for our sins. He rose from the dead, demonstrating God's approval of the sacrifice and His power over death. Those who place their faith in Him will not perish, but have eternal life.

There are times we may hear different religious ideas and philosophies, but there is one thing we must guard—the truth of the gospel. We must see that the gospel remains in us, unwavering and forever central to the truth of what we believe. In the passage above, the word *remain* is the Greek word *meno*, meaning "to stay, dwell, continue, endure, or tarry." It is the same word Jesus used in speaking to His disciples when He said, "If you remain in me and I in you, you will bear much fruit."[6] And later when He said, "As the Father has loved me, so have I loved you. Now remain in my love. If you keep my commands, you will remain in my love, just as I have kept my Father's commands and remain in his love."[7] Do you sense God's desire for continual fellowship? He desires for us to abide with Him. He wants His love to dwell in us, and now we read from John that the truth or message of the gospel ought to abide continually in us.

How does that look in a practical sense? Certainly it means to remain firmly grounded in the basic truth of the gospel, not allowing anyone to lead you astray. On a more personal note, I have made it a regular practice to reflect on the gospel message and thank the Lord for His kindness toward me daily. Typically when I pray, I start off by praising God for who He is—for His power, His majesty, His wisdom, His sovereignty. As I do that, I recognize my sin and unworthiness before a holy God. I confess my sin, which leads me to a point of thanking Him for all He has done for me: sending His Son as payment on my behalf, cleansing me and transforming me, sending His Spirit to live inside of me. In this way the gospel remains in me, at the forefront of my thoughts each day.

As I revisit the gospel in gratitude each day, my heart overflows with joy. That joy spills out in love toward other people. One day I was praying and walking on the golf course at the local country club. I was reflecting on the gospel message and I must admit a smile burst on my face as a direct result of my joy-filled Jesus thoughts. Now when I walk on the course I go out before the golfers get there, but the greens keepers are always busy getting things ready for the day. I know most of them because I see them on a regular basis. One day there was a new worker, and for the first time I realized that my big, bright, genuine smile might seem slightly odd to the casual observer. I saw the man go over and whisper to his friend. He pointed to me and motioned like someone who was drinking, as if to say the only reason I would have such a smile on my face was because I was under the influence! Oh, my—I think I was slightly misunderstood!

It made me think of the verse, "Do not be drunk with wine...but be filled with the Spirit."[8] I guess when we reflect on the goodness of the Lord and the message of the gospel, we are filled with an elixir of joy that no one can take away!

> *Thank You, Father, for the joy that the gospel brings to our hearts. Simply to remember that we were dead in our sins, but You chose to make us alive in Christ makes us overwhelmingly grateful. May this great truth continually be my source of joy each day.*

The Teacher

At my kids' school there was always a scramble each year by the moms trying to figure out how to get their children in the favorite teacher's class for the next grade level. They would try to do whatever they could to get their kids in the "best teacher's" class. In college the scramble continued as students tried to go online at midnight to get the classes with the most gifted or desirable professors. A gifted, knowledgeable, and caring teacher makes all the difference. It is good to know that our heavenly Father has given us the best teacher in the universe—the Holy Spirit. As Jesus was getting ready to leave this earth He told His disciples, "The Holy Spirit, whom the Father will send in my name, will teach you all things and will remind you of everything I have said to you."[9]

The unction, or anointing, of the Holy Spirit dwells in us. His presence lights our path and helps us to understand God's truth. Just as John warned about the false teachers, he also reassured the believers about the true Teacher:

1 JOHN 2:26-27

I am writing these things to you about those who are trying to lead you astray. As for you, the anointing you received from him remains in you, and you do not need anyone to teach you. But as his anointing teaches you about all things and as that anointing is real, not counterfeit—just as it has taught you, remain in him.

John is not saying that we don't need any teachers now that we have the Holy Spirit. That would be a dangerous thing to say, and it would discount the spiritual gift of teaching, which is mentioned several times in the New Testament. If we look at this verse in context, John was warning about false teachers, so he continued by reminding the believers to let the Holy Spirit guide their understanding and give them discernment. He was reminding them that they were not ignorant pupils who needed some extra enlightenment. Remember Cerinthus? He claimed to have special knowledge and enlightenment that he had received from the angels. John is saying, you don't need this supposed teaching from angels or from an enlightened person who claims to get his knowledge from some special source. The Holy Spirit is the one who teaches us.

It is interesting how many cults and sects and even some major religions today claim to have messages from angels as an extra form of enlightenment. Be alert and be careful! Be on your guard against false religions and false beliefs. Allow the truth of the gospel to remain as your solid foundation, and remember that the Holy Spirit is your teacher, not someone who claims to have gotten an extrabiblical message from angels. Remember that Satan comes as a messenger of light.

Now, don't get me wrong as far as angels are concerned. Certainly angels have been used by God and we see references to them throughout Scripture. We must appreciate the work of angels, but we should not worship them or claim some sort of secret knowledge or enlightenment from them.

Interestingly, Paul also warned about those who claim to have special teaching from angels. In his letter to the Colossians he wrote,

> *Do not let anyone who delights in false humility and the worship of angels disqualify you. Such a person also goes into great detail about what they have seen; they are puffed up with idle notions by their unspiritual mind. They have lost connection with the head, from whom the whole body, supported and held together by its ligaments and sinews, grows as God causes it to grow.* [10]

We don't want to lose connection from the head, as Paul was saying. We want to remain connected! As we remain in Christ, dwelling in His Word, rejoicing in the truth of the gospel, and connecting with Him in prayer, we aren't walking around headless! We are not deceived by empty and hollow philosophies. Instead we grow in the truth and in confidence. As His Spirit directs us and opens our eyes toward His truth, we are able to discern the counterfeit from the truth; or should we say a spiritually loaded chocolate pie from the real deal!

Unashamed

It's amazing the length people will go in order to avoid shame and embarrassment. Recently, a story in the news caught my eye. A female law student had been too ashamed to tell her parents she had been kicked out of law school for her low grades. Sadly, she had spent more time socializing than studying and the consequences had finally caught up with her. She couldn't face disappointing her parents, so she made up an elaborate story about a guy who followed her home, held her at gunpoint, and raped her. She kept her story going for eight days, even after police arrested a man who fit her description. Eventually her lie was exposed, and she faced even greater public humiliation and shame in the courtroom than she ever would have faced with her parents. She now faces a two-year sentence in a detention facility.

What makes a person create such an elaborate story? In the case of our misguided law student, she was too ashamed to tell her parents about her failure to do what she was supposed to be doing. Shame is what we feel when our unrighteous or displeasing acts are exposed. Way back in the Garden of Eden, Adam and Eve felt shame before the Lord because they had disobeyed Him. David felt shame when his sin with Bathsheba was exposed by Nathan. Peter felt shame when the cock crowed after he had denied Christ three times. It's not so much in the doing of the act that we feel ashamed—it is when we get caught by someone we love and respect. The fear of being ashamed can have a sanctifying effect. It makes us want to do what is right and pursue righteousness.

If the young law student had communicated with her parents all along the way, telling them she was struggling with her grades and seeking their counsel and help, there wouldn't have been any need for her to be ashamed. Communication and participation together help prevent needless embarrassment down the road. Staying connected is key in any healthy relationship and builds confidence, not shame, between the parties. John continually encouraged the early believers to stay connected with Christ. When we abide in Him, dwelling in Him and remaining in Him, we have confidence in Him, because we turn to Him in our weakness and seek His strength. We confess our sins and enjoy the beauty of His forgiveness and a oneness in our relationship.

When Christ appears, we don't want to be embarrassed or ashamed before Him. John wrote to this end, offering the perfect solution:

1 JOHN 2:28

Now, dear children, continue in him, so that when he appears
we may be confident and unashamed before him at his coming.

To "continue in him" means to walk with Christ in close fellowship. It means more than just saying a quick prayer at dinner or at church. It means walking closely with Him throughout your day. It includes confessing your sins and sharing your struggles with Him, seeking His help to live in obedience to Him. It also means remaining in His love and allowing His love to flow through you and bless those around you. If we walk in fellowship with Him, we will in no way be ashamed when He appears. We can be confident, because He is not some holy stranger or far-off God before whom we would cower in fear. No, as we walk in fellowship with Him, we look forward to seeing our loving Savior return, because we have a joyful relationship with Him.

It's like welcoming home a dear friend you have been communicating with for years. You are close and there are no secrets. You look forward to seeing one another because your love and respect have developed over the years. The more we walk with Jesus, the more we love Him and come to understand His rich mercy and grace toward us. We anticipate His coming with joy and not shame because we have been open with Him about our weaknesses and our needs and have sought His help all along the way.

Visible Proof

When I was in high school I sang in my church choir. Now this wasn't just any choir—this was the chapel choir of First Baptist Church in downtown Dallas. We were no small group. There were about 200 of us high-schoolers in the choir, and every summer we took incredible trips, singing in nations all over the world. My favorite trip was during the United States bicentennial year, 1976. Our trip started in Washington DC, then we went on to Philadelphia for the Fourth of July parade, in which we sang as we marched. Next, we flew to Paris where we actually sang in the halls of Notre Dame and Versailles. We made our way through Europe, stopping in London and Vienna and at several military bases in Germany.

We had uniforms for every occasion. Our performance costumes were outfits from the time of the Revolutionary War—the guys wore white knickers with red long coats and blue triangular hats, while we girls wore long colonial dresses with Betsy Ross caps on our heads. We were quite a stunning bunch marching through the streets of Philadelphia for the bicentennial parade! Now can you imagine what it was like traveling with 200 kids across the globe? It was a monumental task just to keep track of us. The solution was, we not only had our performance costumes, but we also had uniforms for sightseeing and traveling in order to be easily spotted. Try to picture 100 girls walking through the streets of Europe, all dressed in the same striped shirt and white pants. It was always obvious to onlookers that we were part of a group.

When it comes to following Christ, it ought to be obvious that we belong to Him as well. People should be able to spot a follower of Christ by certain traits. Throughout John's epistle he mentions different behaviors that should identify a Christian. One of those identifying factors is living a righteous life. He wrote,

1 John 2:29

If you know that he is righteous, you know that everyone who does what is right has been born of him.

We look like we belong to Christ when we live a righteous life. Our obedience to God demonstrates our love for God. Nathanael Emmons put it this way: "Obedience to God is the most infallible evidence of sincere and supreme love to Him."[11] Perhaps John himself was reflecting back to the last few hours before the cross, when Jesus told His disciples, "If you love Me, you will keep My commandments."[12] If we love Him we want to be identified as one of His. The beautiful truth is that Jesus didn't simply tell us to obey Him and leave it at that. He added, "I will ask the Father, and he will give you another advocate to help you and be with you forever—the Spirit of truth."[13]

Isn't it wonderful to know that we are not alone in trying to live a righteous life? On our own we stumble and fall in our attempt to live in obedience to Him, but God in His kindness sent His Spirit to live in us and dwell among us. In the Psalms we are told, "The LORD directs the steps of the godly. He delights in every detail of their lives. Though they stumble, they will never fall, for the LORD holds them by the hand."[14]

Corrie ten Boom was a strong and godly Dutch woman who was sent to the Nazi concentration camps during World War II because she had helped hide Jewish people from the Nazi invaders. She knew she was not alone in her struggle to do what was right. Her help came from God's Spirit within her and not her own strength and power. After the war, she spoke to many audiences about her faith in Christ and the trials she faced in the concentration camps. Sometimes when she spoke she used the illustration of a glove to make her point: "I have a glove here in my hand. The glove cannot do anything by itself, but when my hand is in it, it can do many things. True, it is not the glove, but my hand in the glove that acts. We are gloves. It is the Holy Spirit in us who is the hand, who does the job. We have to make room for the hand so that every finger is filled."

What beautiful things we "gloves" can do when filled with the Lord's hand! As we allow Him to live and work through us, we can love even our enemies. We can courageously stand up for what is right. We can reach out in kindness and compassion. We can genuinely love our brothers and sisters. We can bring glory and honor to Him.

> *Father, fill our lives and make us useful vessels for Your kingdom. Pour Your love through us, and let us live obedient and righteous lives, bringing You glory.*

Getting Personal

ABIDING TRUTH:

- The Holy Spirit abides in you as a believer, and He leads you into the truth.

- The gospel of Jesus Christ is a sure foundation.

- See that the gospel remains in your heart and mind.

- Reflecting on the gospel brings great joy to our lives.

- Be aware of false teachers.

- God has given us the best Teacher. Seek the Holy Spirit's guidance in discerning truth.

- Walk with Christ, communicating with Him throughout your day.

- Allow God's Spirit to help you live a righteous life.

ADDITIONAL READING: Colossians 2

ACTION STEPS: Everyday thank-you

John encourages us to let the gospel message remain in us continually. As I mentioned in the chapter, one way we can do this is by taking a moment each day to thank the Lord Jesus for offering His life for our sake. I often think of the precious prayer, "Father, thank You for having mercy on a sinner like me." What a beautiful truth to reflect on in gratitude each day! May we never allow our hearts to grow cold or forget the beauty of the gospel. "I once was lost, but now am found, was blind but now I see." Amazing grace—how sweet the sound!

Make it a habit to reflect on the gospel message and thank God every day for the fact that although you were dead in your sins, you have been made alive in Christ by faith in what He did on the cross. Write out a prayer of gratitude for what Christ has done for you.

_____

_____

_____

_____

_____

CHAPTER SIX

$\mathcal{L}$avishly Loved by Him

*True love begins
when nothing is looked for in return.*
ANTOINE DE SAINT-EXUPÉRY

*"To all who did receive him,
to those who believed in his name,
he gave the right to become children of God."*
JOHN 1:12

Beth Gotwalt passionately lives the life she didn't plan. She never pictured herself as a mother of an autistic son, but life doesn't always take the path we intended. Often there are unexpected twists and turns, and we can learn and grow through our experiences. One of the greatest areas of growth for any parent is in the area of self-less and unconditional love, but the parent of an autistic child will probably find herself especially stretched. Beth's love for her son is a testimony of how wide our hearts can expand to love and embrace

99

someone who doesn't fit into the perfect little box of human expectations.

There are many stories Beth could share about trying moments or difficult fixes she has experienced as a result of having a child with autism, but she doesn't focus on the trials, she focuses on the blessings. Although raising an autistic child has profound challenges, Beth's love for her son runs deeper still. I asked her to share one of her joyful experiences with you.

As a mother of a child with autism, I love my child like all mothers love their children. And yet, Tanner adds a different dimension. He is like a 2-year-old in a 15-year-old body in many ways. It is not always easy to be his mom, but there are so many moments that he brings such joy to my heart. These moments of joy make it so easy to love him!

A few years ago, we were attending my oldest son, Adam's, cross-country meet at a large park. It was a district meet and there were hundreds of people everywhere. Tanner and I found a nice spot away from the crowd where we could sit quietly and wait for Adam to run. I had only brought one chair, so Tanner was sitting in my lap. He was 11 years old at the time. Tanner was content to listen to his music, but then something got his attention. He had turned to look at me and caught his reflection in my sunglasses. He loves to look at himself in the mirror and make faces, so he started looking into my glasses and making all these hilarious and funny faces. It just made me laugh. And laugh. And laugh! He wasn't trying to make me laugh, he was just amusing himself. It was a completely spontaneous and funny moment. I wondered how strange we must look. A woman sitting in a chair with her pre-adolescent son on her lap making faces into her glasses. Yet, right then, I grabbed that moment and took complete delight in my son.

I think that is a perfect example of *agape* love. Taking

delight in the things our loved ones do, no matter how funny or strange it might be. Tanner is so good at teaching me to stop and savor a moment, a word, or a phrase. In these moments, I truly believe that God is loving me through my delight in Tanner![1]

Beth's all-encompassing love for and delight in her son offers a glimpse into the type of love God lavishes upon us. His love is a delight-filled love that doesn't give up; that's how I would describe the love Beth demonstrates day in and day out with her son. In a similar way, God's love toward us is steadfast and enduring. It is abundant and unending. It's difficult to comprehend His love because it is greater than any human demonstration of love we see on this earth. Powerful and patient. Undeserved and gracious. Oh, if only we could begin to understand how deep and wide God's love is for His people!

David seemed to have unique and heartfelt appreciation for God's steadfast love, and we often read his descriptions of God's relentless love in the Psalms. Perhaps his understanding of God's love developed as he spent time with the Lord alone in the wilderness, watching his father's flock. Maybe it came about as he sat in wonder at the vast expanse of stars that illuminated the night sky with such majesty and brilliance. Certainly his faith and dependence on God's love grew as David depended on Him to help him escape his enemies and fight off predators. But I think David grew to understand God's love most as he experienced His kind mercy and forgiveness toward his sin.

Consider some of the ways David proclaimed God's generous love:

> *Your love, LORD, reaches to the heavens,*
> *your faithfulness to the skies.*
> *Your righteousness is like the highest mountains,*
> *your justice like the great deep.*
> *You, LORD, preserve both people and animals.*
> *How priceless is your unfailing love, O God!*
> *People take refuge in the shadow of your wings.*

They feast on the abundance of your house;
  you give them drink from your river of delights.
For with you is the fountain of life;
  in your light we see light. [2]

I have seen you in your sanctuary
  and gazed upon your power and glory.
Your unfailing love is better than life itself;
  how I praise you! [3]

As high as the heavens are above the earth,
  so great is his love for those who fear him;
as far as the east is from the west,
  so far has he removed our transgressions from us.
As a father has compassion on his children,
  so the LORD *has compassion on those who fear him.* [4]

Praise the LORD.
Give thanks to the LORD, *for he is good;*
  his love endures forever. [5]

David went beyond merely knowing about God's love—it was a part of his very being. He seemed to understand the Father's love in all of its fullness. In Psalm 136, we see the phrase "His love endures forever" repeated 26 times!

In some translations the word *love* is rendered *mercy*. In others it is termed *unfailing love* or *lovingkindness*, or in *The Message* (a modern paraphrase) we find "His love never quits." The original Hebrew word is actually the unique and beautiful term *hesed*.

Hesed is a very rich word; filled with a wealth of meaning and truth. It is considered by many biblical scholars to be one of the most important terms in Old Testament theology and ethics. It has three basic meanings, which all interact together: "strength," "steadfastness," and "love." The word *hesed* cannot be fully understood unless all three of the meanings are incorporated. Generally, the English word *love* connotes a bit of lighthearted, fluffy affection, but when we put *love* together with *steadfastness* and *strength* we begin to understand the enduring nature of *hesed*-type love.

Hesed implies loyalty and mercy. It also implies personal involvement and a covenant between two parties beyond what the law requires. For example, a husband and wife are legally bound to each other, yet their relationship transcends the legal document and represents a bond and commitment between the two of them. The prophet Hosea spoke of this covenant love, or *hesed,* between God and His people: "I will betroth you to me forever; I will betroth you in righteousness and justice, in love and compassion. I will betroth you in faithfulness, and you will acknowledge the LORD."[6]

God showed His *hesed* for his beloved children, uniting Himself with them as a bridegroom to a bride. There was an expectation that a mutual love existed between the two. Not only did God demonstrate this enduring love and kindness to His own, but He also wanted them to know and understand His *hesed* love for them. Much more than head-knowledge, God desired for His people to *embrace* His *hesed* love. Consider the words He spoke through the prophet Jeremiah:

> *This is what the LORD says:*
> *"Let not the wise boast of their wisdom*
>   *or the strong boast of their strength*
>   *or the rich boast of their riches,*
> *but let the one who boasts boast about this:*
>   *that they have the understanding to know me,*
>   *that I am the Lord, who exercises kindness [hesed],*
>   *justice and righteousness on earth,*
>   *for in these I delight,"*
> *declares the LORD.*[7]

Agape Love

Wisdom, strength (power), and riches are all areas in which humans tend to boast and find their strength. But Jeremiah tells us if we are going to boast in one thing, we should boast in the fact that we know and understand that God exercises justice, righteousness, and *hesed* love toward us! *Hesed* portrays His love for His people in a persistent and powerful way in the Old Testament. In the New Testament (which was written in Greek) we see another word identifying God's love. The Greek language has several different words for love: *eros,* which is sensual or passionate love; *philia,* which represents brotherly love; and *storge,* which denotes a natural affection. Yet it is the term *agape* that expresses a strong, altruistic, and sacrificial God-type love.

The apostle Paul elaborated on *agape* love in his first letter to the Corinthians. Perhaps you are familiar with his description:

> *Love is patient, love is kind. It does not envy, it does not boast, it is not proud. It does not dishonor others, it is not self-seeking, it is not easily angered, it keeps no record of wrongs. Love does not delight in evil but rejoices with the truth. It always protects, always trusts, always hopes, always perseveres. Love never fails.*[8]

What a beautiful picture of how we are loved by God!

Agape love is broader than *hesed* in that it extends toward the undeserving. We see it in John's Gospel when Jesus said, "God so loved the world that he gave his one and only Son, that whoever believes in him shall not perish but have eternal life." Jesus also told us to love (*agape*) our enemies. He himself demonstrated sacrificial love toward those who do not deserve it when He gave His life on the cross for us. The powerful love of Christ was shown toward us in that while we were yet sinners, He died for us.[9] This is true *agape* love, to graciously love those who have not earned it or merited it. Ben Witherington III, a professor of biblical studies at Asbury Theological Seminary, described the *agape* love of 1 Corinthians 13 like this:

> This sort of love has nothing to do with attractiveness or attraction. It is often bestowed on the unloved and the unlovely. It is an expression of grace, which means undeserved and unmerited benefit or favor bestowed on someone. In

a world of reciprocity, and "you scratch my back, and I'll scratch yours," such love seems to break the cycle of payback, and reaches a person as a true gift, one that comes without strings attached. This is the greater agape the Bible refers to, and it is surely no exaggeration to say that it is a love humans are not capable of apart from divine example, assistance and enablement.[10]

We tend to throw the word *love* around to mean all sorts of frivolous things: "Oh, I love your new outfit!" "I love cake-mix-flavored frozen yogurt with sprinkles on top." "I love the beach." "I love this new book!" What we typically mean is that we really, really like something or feel a surface-level affection for it. Sometimes we equate love with how we've been treated by a parent or a friend or spouse. But God's love is beyond what we see in human affection. When we examine the definition of love that Paul gave us, we see a love whose definition comes from beyond this world. We can scarcely begin to comprehend the depth of God's love. Earthly comparisons of altruistic love leave us lacking in the understanding of the height and breadth of the love of God.

Author and pastor Chip Ingram writes,

> God's holy disposition is directed toward all that he has created, not just the good or the obedient. The source of this loving disposition is in God, not the object. We don't provoke, trick, convince, earn, or win God's love. He doesn't love us because of who we are but because of who he is. His nature and character compel him to express unconditional affection toward us.[11]

My friend, even in our ugliness, our sinfulness, our foolishness, God loves us with an unending *agape* love.

His love is unchangeable, unfailing, unstoppable, unrelenting, unending, unaffordable, unfathomable. It is faithful, forever, and true. Because of His love He pursues us, purifies us, protects us, comforts us, cares for us, and corrects us. His love is perfect and complete.

Generous Love

We can't afford God's love, but He gives it to us freely. He is not stingy in the way He bestows His love on us—rather, He is generous. John desired that Christ's followers would sense how wonderfully loved they are by the Father. To God's beloved children (those who trust in Him) John wrote,

1 JOHN 3:1

See what great love the Father has lavished on us, that we should be called children of God! And that is what we are!

Lavished! Did you catch that word? Lavished: bestowed profusely. God is not guarded or restrained when it comes to His love for us. His love pours out in generous measure. Stop and drink this truth from John into your heart. Allow it to permeate your being. You are lavishly loved with the sincerest, most powerful love imaginable. A *hesed* love: strong, steadfast, merciful, loyal, patient, enduring love. A love that does not stop, does not end—we cannot step out of it or away from it. Its strength overwhelms. If only we lived each day engulfed in the knowledge of His great love for us!

The apostle Paul prayed that believers would grasp how wide and long and high and deep the love of Christ is toward His own.[12] He wanted us to know God's love, which surpasses knowledge. He was convinced that neither death nor life, neither angels nor demons, neither the present nor the future, nor any powers, neither height nor depth, nor anything else in all creation, would be able to separate us from the love of God that is in Christ Jesus our Lord.[13]

What does this kind of undeserved, abundant love do to us? When we realize it—I mean, when we really begin to get a glimpse of how sincerely loved we are—it changes us. We live in confidence. We live with gratitude. We live with a desire to please the One who so lavishly loves us. We live with joy, with hope, with strength, with peace. Knowing we are recipients of such generous love, we in turn love others more sincerely. We forgive others more readily, and we graciously overlook annoyances. Most important, we love our Father in return because He so richly loves us.

If we don't live like this, why is it? Could it be that we do not comprehend His great love for us? Is it possible that we grow so busy in our day that we do not take the time to reflect upon it? Could it be that we are simply so distracted by what seems to fulfill us that we forget the only fulfilling and complete love is His love for us? Take a moment to stop and reflect on His generous love right now.

> *Father, we are overwhelmed by Your loving-kindness and tender mercies toward us. We are so undeserving, but You are so mighty and great. We relish Your steadfast love and receive it willingly. All we can do is whisper, "Thank You."*

His Kids

The word *father* is a wonderful term of endearment. Old Testament prophets and saints honored God as El-Elyon (God Most High) or El-Shaddai (God Almighty), and Jehovah-Jireh (God will Provide). Certainly these are descriptive of our God and King, but John helps us understand our relationship to God through Christ. Those who have received Christ have been given the right to be called "children of God." What an amazing honor! God is not a distant being—He is our Abba Father (our Daddy), and we are His beloved children. As believers in Christ we have a privileged position, for we are a part of His family.

In Romans we read, "The Spirit you received does not make you slaves, so that you live in fear again; rather, the Spirit you received brought about your adoption to sonship. And by him we cry, *'Abba, Father.'* The Spirit himself testifies with our spirit that we are God's children."[14] Believers in Christ have the honor and privilege of being called God's children. We are a part of His family.

John Phillips wrote, "Our Father! It is, indeed, the greatest of all names for God, a name that demonstrates that He loves us. More—He loves us enough to make us His children, to put us in His family."[15] Thomas Watson took this thought even further in saying, "Since God has a Son of His own, and such a Son; how wonderful God's love in adopting us! We needed a Father, but He did not need sons."[16] Who are we that the God of all creation would want to be our Daddy? It is astonishing, isn't it? That God would so choose to adopt us into His family and call us His own.

As His children, how do we respond to such love? How should we behave as a part of God's family? Shouldn't we look a little different from the rest of the world? The apostle John pointed out some distinct differences in family resemblance:

1 JOHN 3:1-10

The reason the world does not know us is that it did not know him. Dear friends, now we are children of God, and what we will be has not yet been made known. But we know that when Christ appears, we shall be like him, for we shall see him as he is. All who have this hope in him purify themselves, just as he is pure.

Everyone who sins breaks the law; in fact, sin is lawlessness. But you know that he appeared so that he might take away our sins. And in him is no sin. No one who lives in him keeps on sinning. No one who continues to sin has either seen him or known him.

Dear children, do not let anyone lead you astray. The one who does what is right is righteous, just as he is righteous. The one who does what is sinful is of the devil, because the devil has been sinning from the beginning. The reason the Son of God appeared was to destroy the devil's work. No one who is born of God will continue to sin, because God's seed remains in them; they cannot go on sinning, because they have been born of God. This is how we know who the children of God are and who the children of the devil are: Anyone who does not do what is right

*is not God's child, nor is anyone who does not love their brother
and sister.*

John makes it crystal clear that God's children look different than
those who do not follow Him. He begins by reminding us that the
world will not know or appreciate (Greek word for "know," *ginosko,*
implies the idea of appreciation) who we are because they don't know
who Christ is. In a similar line of thought concerning Jesus, John wrote
in his Gospel, "He was in the world, and though the world was made
through him, the world did not recognize him."[17] So if the world did
not recognize and appreciate God's only begotten Son, the world most
likely won't appreciate the other family members either.

God's children have other family traits as well. John says they will
not keep on sinning. God is righteous, and since we are a part of his
family we ought to look like our Daddy. John goes further to say that
if we are God's children we will also love our brothers and sisters—a
reoccurring theme throughout his letter. Hatred among brothers and
sisters simply has no place in God's family.

Present and future are both mentioned in this passage. We currently
are God's children as believers in Christ, and He is continuing to do
a work in us. One day in the future when He appears, we shall be like
Him, in a glorified body. This is the second time in John's letter that he
mentions Jesus will appear again. Although we do not know when He
will appear, we know that He will return. John refers to Christ's second
coming several times in this epistle, and of course we read his description of the return of Christ in the book of Revelation.[18]

In Philippians the apostle Paul wrote about the transformation we
will experience at Christ's coming, saying, "Our citizenship is in heaven.
And we eagerly await a Savior from there, the Lord Jesus Christ, who,
by the power that enables him to bring everything under his control,
will transform our lowly bodies so that they will be like his glorious
body."[19] Oh, what a glorious future we have! May we live our lives to
honor Him as we anticipate that glorious day when we shall be with
Him face-to-face, and we shall see Him as He is.

In her popular devotional *Jesus Calling*, author Sarah Young wrote an entry based on 1 John 3:2. Here's how she put it from Jesus' perspective:

> You are a child of God, and you are Mine forever…Since you are part of My royal family, you're a fellow-heir with Me—sharing My inheritance. However, you must share My suffering if you are to share My Glory. You don't need to search for ways to suffer. Living in this broken world provides ample opportunity to experience pain of many kinds. When adversity comes your way, search for Me in the midst of your struggles. Ask Me to help you suffer well, in a manner worthy of royalty. Everything you endure can help you become more like Me. Remember the ultimate goal: You will see My Face in righteousness—and be satisfied![20]

Do What Is Right

John wrote "The one who does what is right is righteous, just as he is righteous." And later he pointed out that the one who does *not* do what is right is *not* God's child. What does he mean by doing what is right? Does he mean obeying the Ten Commandments? Does he mean living in constant obedience to Jesus? Does he mean reading God's Word and obeying it? Does he mean selling everything we have and giving it to the poor? It is important for us to grasp what John was aiming at here, and we must use God's Word to help us interpret this passage.

The Bible says that there is none righteous, no, not one. It tells us that all have sinned and fallen short of His glory. Although we are sinners and have disobeyed God in a variety of ways, we are made righteous through Christ. Righteousness is a gracious gift of God to those who believe in Christ. Through Him we are brought into a right relationship with God. Righteousness is unattainable on our own by trying to obey the law. We will always fall short. Yet, when we place our faith in Christ we become the righteousness of God in Him. Paul wrote to the Corinthians, "God made him who had no sin [Jesus] to be sin for us, so that in him we might become the righteousness of God."[21]

Paul wrote to the Galatians,

We know that a person is made right with God by faith in Jesus Christ, not by obeying the law. And we have believed in Christ Jesus, so that we might be made right with God because of our faith in Christ, not because we have obeyed the law. For no one will ever be made right with God by obeying the law.[22]

We have been made right with God because of Jesus' righteousness, not our own. John also makes it clear that if we are in Christ we will not continue in sin. He didn't mean we won't ever sin, but he did say that we won't keep on practicing sin or habitually live in sin. A follower of Christ won't live in continual sin because the power of sin no longer has a hold on her life. Paul wrote in Corinthians that God provides a way to escape when we are tempted. We all experience temptations, but we are not left alone to try to escape. Here's how Paul put it:

The temptations in your life are no different from what others experience. And God is faithful. He will not allow the temptation to be more than you can stand. When you are tempted, he will show you a way out so that you can endure.[23]

A true follower of Christ cannot go on sinning because she has the Spirit of God living in her. John's words are clear and straightforward: "No one who is born of God will continue to sin, because God's seed remains in them; they cannot go on sinning, because they have been born of God." Knowing we are lavishly and sincerely loved by Him makes us want to live a righteous life, just like a woman who knows she is sincerely loved by her husband wants to please him and do what honors him. It's God's kindness and love that draw us to repentance and a desire to live a righteous life. Never underestimate the power of love!

When We Don't Feel Loved

There are times when we doubt God's love because He doesn't seem to answer our earnest prayers. He seems to wait or hesitate, and sometimes we may think He is not listening at all. Let us not think that because He delays, His love is diminished. Quite the contrary—His great love for us may cause Him to delay because He knows what is best for us. The following thoughts are from a timeless devotional called *Streams in the Desert.* Originally published in 1925, its truths continue to speak to our hearts today. I wanted to share this entry with you since it is based on the inspired words of John written in his Gospel.

It centers on the story of Jesus' dear friends Mary, Martha, and Lazarus. As you may remember, the two sisters, Mary and Martha, sent word to Jesus that their brother, Lazarus, was sick. Instead of rushing to His friends to heal him, Jesus waited several days, and by the time He finally arrived Lazarus was already dead. You can imagine it would have been easy for the two sisters to doubt Jesus' genuine love for them when He had chosen to not come immediately. Consider how the writer of this devotion addressed the question of love that waits.

> "When he [Jesus] had heard therefore that he was sick, he abode two days still in the same place where he was" (John 11:6).

> In the forefront of this marvelous chapter stands the affirmation, "Jesus loved Martha, and her sister, and Lazarus," as if to teach us that at the very heart and foundation of all God's dealings with us, however dark and mysterious they may be, we must dare to believe in and assert the infinite, unmerited, and unchanging love of God. Love permits pain. The sisters never doubted that He would speed at all hazards and stay their brother from death, but, "When he had heard therefore that he was sick, he abode two days still in the same place where he was."

> What a startling "therefore"! He abstained from going, not because He did not love them, but because He did love them. His love alone kept Him back from hasting at once to the dear and stricken home. Anything less than infinite

love must have rushed instantly to the relief of those loved and troubled hearts, to stay their grief and to have the luxury of wiping and stanching their tears and causing sorrow and sighing to flee away. Divine love could alone hold back the impetuosity of the Savior's tenderheartedness until the Angel of Pain had done her work.

Who can estimate how much we owe to suffering and pain? But for them we should have little scope for many of the chief virtues of the Christian life. Where were faith, without trial to test it; or patience, with nothing to bear; or experience, without tribulation to develop it?—*Selected*

> "Loved! then the way will not be drear;
> For One we know is ever near,
> Proving it to our hearts so clear
> That we are loved.
> "Loved when our sky is clouded o'er,
> And days of sorrow press us sore;
> Still we will trust Him evermore,
> For we are loved.
> "Time, that affects all things below,
> Can never change the love He'll show;
> The heart of Christ with love will flow,
> And we are loved." [24]

My friend, trust His love for you. Even when it seems He has delayed or isn't listening. Even when your life has turned out differently than you planned. We can trust His love because we can trust His goodness. Chip Ingram adds,

> Ultimately, God isn't good because he does good things for us. And God isn't good because of something in us. God is good because of something in him. He can be nothing else. Both God and his choices remain good, even when they may not feel or look particularly good to you. [25]

Allow your faith in a good God, a *hesed/agape*-loving heavenly Father, to carry you through the storms.

Getting Personal

ABIDING TRUTH:

- God wants us to know and understand His love.
- God's *hesed* love toward us is rich in strength, steadfastness, and mercy.
- *Agape* love (patient, kind, not self-seeking…) describes the Father's love for us.
- God profusely bestows His genuine and perfect love on us.
- Knowing and understanding His love changes us.
- As His beloved children, we walk in obedience.
- Live in anticipation of the glorious day when we shall see Him face-to-face.
- Trust His love in times of waiting.

ADDITIONAL READING: Psalm 136

ACTION STEPS: Love note to God

Take some time alone to be still and dwell upon simply one thought—the love of the Father. Consider all that we have learned in this chapter about His loving-kindness and tender mercies toward us. His enduring and pure love toward us as His children is an overwhelming thought to contemplate. Just be still and drench yourself in the thought of His joyful and redeeming love for you personally. He sent His Son so you could become a part of His family. What sacrifice! What love!

After you have spent some quiet time alone with Him, write out a loving response to Him, telling Him how you love Him. You may use the lines below or begin a love journal. Consider making it a consistent practice to reflect on His love and write Him notes in return.

_____

_____

_____

_____

_____

_____

_____

_____

PART FOUR

Recognizing Real Faith

*"If we would know whether our faith is genuine,
we do well to ask ourselves how we are living."*

J.C. RYLE

*"The Holy Spirit produces this kind of fruit in our lives:
love, joy, peace, patience, kindness,
goodness, faithfulness,
gentleness, and self-control.
There is no law against these things!
Those who belong to Christ Jesus
have nailed the passions and desires
of their sinful nature to his cross and crucified them
there. Since we are living by the Spirit, let us follow the
Spirit's leading in every part of our lives."*

GALATIANS 5:22-25 NLT

$\mathcal{B}$old Confidence

*"The primary test of life is not service but love,
both for man and for God."*

WILLIAM STILL

*"Jesus replied: 'Love the Lord your God
with all your heart and with all your soul
and with all your mind.' This is the first
and greatest commandment.
And the second is like it: 'Love your neighbor as yourself.'
All the Law and the Prophets hang on
these two commandments."*

MATTHEW 22:37-40

When we jumped out of our SUV in downtown Dallas we didn't know who we would encounter or what type of people they would be. You never know what to expect when you go to feed the homeless. It's a different story every time. On this particularly crisp fall day we were bringing food to hand out with our friend Rip Parker. Rip dedicated his life to feeding the homeless in downtown

Dallas, going every day of the week to hand out sandwiches made with donated food from area restaurants and churches. Known affectionately as "the Rev" (short for *Reverend*)because of his love for Jesus, Rip faithfully visited several different locations where he knew the homeless men and women hung out. Occasionally on a Sunday afternoon we would join Rip as a family to help him serve sandwiches and water.

This is a simple story really, but I will never forget it. My daughter Grace (a young teen at the time) had brought her brand-new Bible, which she had just received from us for her birthday. She was particularly excited about it and had carefully picked out just the right cover and type she wanted. As she jumped out of the SUV for our first stop with Rip, Grace began talking with a homeless man who seemed particularly sad. She talked to him about the love of God and His kindness toward us. The man said he knew a little bit about Jesus, but hadn't really read much of the Bible, although he loved to read.

It was then that I could see it all over Grace's face—the realization that she had a new Bible right there in the car. She went straight over and grabbed her new Bible and handed it to the man. His soiled fingers touched the pages with a sense of awe and gratitude. I couldn't believe what I was seeing—her new Bible that was so valuable to her! She was giving it to this lonely and dirty stranger. This was not an easy gift for Grace to give, but she knew his need for it was greater than her own. I must admit—and I'm embarrassed to tell you this—I'm not so sure I would have given away *my* brand-new birthday gift.

This man had no books, no special Bible to call his own until that day Grace gave him hers. I watched her face as she handed him the Bible. She had a few tears rolling down her face. She may have been sensitive because it was hard to give something away that she had wanted and waited for, something she valued. She may have been moved by the desperate need she saw in the face of the man. Actually, I have a feeling the tears were a little of both sadness and joy—sadness for the man and the loss of something special, but also joy over the opportunity to meet a need in someone's life.

It's not easy to give sacrificially. By definition, sacrificial giving requires offering something of value, and that's painful. It wasn't easy for Grace to give away her new Bible, but on the other hand it brought her a great sense of blessing to know that this man would have a beautiful Bible to read, a treasure to keep and to value. I was so proud of her. She showed a true sense of the kind of love that goes far beyond pity. She showed a kind of love that puts another's needs in front of her own desires. Love comes in a variety of shapes and sizes, but I'm proud of Grace for demonstrating sacrificial love that day. Amazing what we can learn from our teenagers.

∞

To love in a sacrificial way makes us vulnerable. It is much safer to hold on to our love and caring and never open our heart up to anyone. Love means taking a risk. It means living selflessly instead of selfishly. You've heard it said: "Better to have loved and lost than never to have loved at all." Love means laying our heart out there—it can even go as far as laying down our rights. But in today's world we tend to run away from difficulties, pain, and heartache. We play it safe when it comes to love and life.

C.S. Lewis pointedly wrote,

> There is no safe investment. To love at all is to be vulnerable. Love anything and your heart will certainly be wrung and possibly be broken. If you want to make sure of keeping it intact, you must give your heart to no one, not even to an animal. Wrap it carefully round with hobbies and little luxuries; avoid all entanglements; lock it up safe in the casket or coffin of your selfishness. But in that casket—safe, dark, motionless, airless—it will change. It will not be broken; it will become unbreakable, impenetrable, irredeemable. The alternative to tragedy, or at least to the risk of tragedy, is damnation. The only place outside heaven where you can be perfectly safe from all the dangers and perturbations of love is Hell.[1]

Aren't We All Lovely?

I suppose most of us would consider ourselves "loving people" to some extent. Not too many people (at least not the thoughtful and kind women who are reading this book) would categorize themselves as "hateful" or "unloving." No, for the most part, people see themselves as identifying more with love than with hate. Up to this point in the book we have read John's reminders about "not hating our brothers and sisters" and have most likely thought that these words were meant for some other reader, one who struggles with hatred, not us. Yet John is about to paint a picture to show us what true love really looks like, and it might be interesting for each one of us to discover where we fit in the portrait.

Just as an artist often begins his painting with large, broad brush-strokes to fill in a backdrop for his scene, so John begins this section of the letter by using the broad terms of *hatred* and *love* to illustrate his point. Here's how he starts out:

1 JOHN 3:11-15

This is the message you heard from the beginning: We should love one another. Do not be like Cain, who belonged to the evil one and murdered his brother. And why did he murder him? Because his own actions were evil and his brother's were righteous. Do not be surprised, my brothers and sisters, if the world hates you. We know that we have passed from death to life, because we love each other. Anyone who does not love remains in death. Anyone who hates a brother or sister is a murderer, and you know that no murderer has eternal life residing in him.

John has already taught us that one distinguishing factor of God's children is that they do what is right. Now he repeats another distinct difference, saying someone who is truly God's child will not hate his brother or sister. John paints this picture in black and white. He wants to be clear because during his day the people were caught up with new knowledge and new information. John kept going back to the clear and basic message the believers had heard when they first came to Christ. He wanted the message they heard from the beginning to remain in them. This message has not changed. There are certain basics of the Christian faith that are unalterable. Here is the message: We should love one another.

So how did he continue to paint a picture to help us see what love looks like? First we examine the contrast of love with hatred—and who was the first to show hatred for his brother? Cain, the son of Adam and Eve. When we read his story in Genesis we are reminded that Cain was jealous because his sacrifice was not accepted by God. His jealousy led to hatred, and hatred to murder. When God accepted Abel's sacrifice and not Cain's, Cain had the opportunity to do what was right—bring an acceptable sacrifice. Yet he did not choose to repent and do the right thing. Instead he murdered the one who did what is right.

Have you ever noticed that unrighteousness can't stand righteousness? Those who want to do what is wrong typically want people to join them in the wrongdoing, and they abhor those who do what is right. This is what Jesus was talking about when He said,

> *Light has come into the world, but people loved darkness instead of light because their deeds were evil. Everyone who does evil hates the light, and will not come into the light for fear that their deeds will be exposed. But whoever lives by the truth comes into the light, so that it may be seen plainly that what they have done has been done in the sight of God.* [2]

We can look at what Cain did and be aghast and think, *How could anyone do such a thing to his brother?* And yet we can look at believers and see bitterness and jealousy pop up in many circles. We see people who hate their brother and sister and even kill their reputation with their stories or words or unkind actions. As I have said before, instead of looking around and pointing the finger at others who seem to exhibit these qualities, let us first examine our own lives and ask God to shine His light on the hatred we may be harboring. We must choose to do what is right and clean house when it comes to hatred, because hatred usually grows into hurting another person in some way, even if it may be only with our words.

Jesus set a high standard in regard to hatred. He said in the Sermon on the Mount, "You have heard that it was said to the people long ago, 'You shall not murder, and anyone who murders will be subject to judgment.' But I tell you that anyone who is angry with a brother or sister will be subject to judgment. Again, anyone who says to a brother or sister, 'Raca ["scoundrel" or "fool"],' is answerable to the court. And anyone who says, 'You fool!' will be in danger of the fire of hell."[3] Ouch! Jesus certainly took anger to a new level of understanding, didn't He? Now it must be understood that Jesus was setting such a high standard that everyone who heard these words would recognize their need for Him. Our passage today must bring us to that same point.

If we are going to allow His love to flourish in our lives, we must first deal with the hatred in our hearts. Let us humbly go to our loving heavenly Father and seek His forgiveness and help in getting rid of it. May we also recognize that our lack of perfection in the area of love continues to remind us of our need for a Savior. Our inability to love and our tendency to hate draw us to the one who is Love. Because He demonstrated His love for us on the cross, we are forgiven when we fall short.

Remember too that if you do what is right and walk in the light, the world will most likely hate you. John reminds the early believers not to be surprised by this hatred. Jesus also warned us not to be surprised: "If you belonged to the world, it would love you as its own. As it is, you do not belong to the world, but I have chosen you out of the world. That is why the world hates you."[4] So we shouldn't be shocked when people hate us for being Christians and standing for what is right. Let us live with love and respond in love to put their hatred to shame. Jesus told us to love our enemies, to do good to those who hate us, to bless those who curse us, and to pray for those who mistreat us. If we show this extraordinary kind of love, then we will be like our Father in heaven, who is kind to the ungrateful and the wicked. Be merciful as your heavenly Father is merciful.

True Love

As John continues to paint a colorful picture of love, he places the focal point in his painting: the one and only image that demonstrates perfectly what love looks like. He gives us the picture of Christ, the One who laid down His life for us. Notice the contrast between one who did what was wrong and took the life of another (illustrated by Cain) and the One who only did what was right and who laid down His life for us:

1 JOHN 3:16

This is how we know what love is: Jesus Christ laid down his life for us. And we ought to lay down our lives for our brothers and sisters.

Ah, what a beautiful portrait indeed! The ultimate picture of true and authentic love! Do you see the strokes of brilliant color as you ponder the portrait of Christ and what He did for us on the cross? The One who knew no sin gave His life on our behalf. Perhaps John was thinking back to the words he heard his beloved Savior say when He described Himself as the good shepherd, "I am the good shepherd. The good shepherd lays down His life for the sheep."[5] Or maybe the apostle was thinking back to Jesus' words just before He faced the cross: "Greater love has no one than this: to lay down one's life for one's friends."[6]

I love the way John says, "This is how we *know* what love is." The word *know* can also be translated *perceive* or *grasp*. Bible commentator Kenneth Wuest described it this way: "The word speaks of knowledge gained by experience. The saints have experienced the love of God in that He laid down His life for them, and in that they have become the recipients of salvation. This knowledge is a permanent possession."[7] As believers in Christ, we have the ability to deeply understand this kind of true love, for we have experienced it ourselves.

Several years ago Curt and I had the privilege of traveling to Paris for business and for pleasure. I of course took him to all the sights I had been to on my high-school choir trip with the chapel choir. I don't think he was as impressed as I was that we had sung in the Cathedral of Notre Dame...oh, well. We also visited places I had not visited on the trip with my 200 choir friends. One of those places was the painter Claude Monet's home in Giverny, France. The delightful tour of his home and gardens brought to life many of the paintings of his I had long admired. We were able to walk through the gardens that were the subject of many of his paintings, and we took pictures by the famous lily-pad pond. We walked where Monet walked and observed the beauty he saw firsthand, with the addition of a few years of growth. Being there in the midst of where the painter had created his masterpieces was an enriching opportunity. Wonderful though it is to see a lovely garden through Monet's eyes, it's another thing to experience it ourselves and sense it in all its beauty.

In a deeper and more personal way, we have not only *heard* stories of the love of Christ, as Christians we have lived it and breathed it. It is part of the very fabric of who we are. We are recipients of His grace, His mercy, and His unfailing love. Commentator John Phillips writes,

> What can we say of *Calvary* love?—which will not let us go and is stronger than death? What can we say of the love that drew salvation's plan and of the grace that brought it down to man? What can we say of that love, which, before time ever began, reached out to lost sinners in all the ages of time? What can we say of that love, which is described thus: "While we were yet sinners, Christ died for us" (Romans 5:8)? When we think of who He is and of what we are, we are simply overwhelmed.[8]

Although our love cannot equal the love of Christ, nor will it accomplish what His love accomplished on the cross, John encourages believers to reflect the love Christ has for us in the way we love our brothers and sisters. We are charged to lay down our lives for them. What does that look like? What does it mean to lay down our lives for others? It means loving others with a sacrificial love, being more concerned about their needs than our own rights and privileges. I'm reminded of how

Paul described the attitude we should have toward others. Using Christ as our example, he wrote,

> *Do nothing out of selfish ambition or vain conceit. Rather, in humility value others above yourselves, not looking to your own interests but each of you to the interests of the others. In your relationships with one another, have the same mindset as Christ Jesus:*
>
> > *Who, being in very nature God,*
> > *did not consider equality with God*
> > *something to be used to*
> > *his own advantage;*
> > *rather, he made himself nothing*
> > *by taking the very nature of a servant,*
> > *being made in human likeness.*
> > *And being found in appearance as a man,*
> > *he humbled himself*
> > *by becoming obedient to death—*
> > *even death on a cross!*
> >
> > *Therefore God exalted him to the highest place*
> > *and gave him the name that is above every name,*
> > *that at the name of Jesus every knee should bow,*
> > *in heaven and on earth and under the earth,*
> > *and every tongue acknowledge that Jesus Christ is Lord,*
> > *to the glory of God the Father.*[9]

As I read this description of love and sacrifice, I'm reminded of how often I selfishly cling to my own way. I'm convicted of the daily battle between my own selfishness and thinking of others' needs more than my own. Jesus didn't cling to His heavenly rights, but made Himself nothing, taking on the very nature of a servant. Laying down our lives means serving our brothers and sisters and thinking of their needs before our own. Sure, we could cling to our status or position, our accomplishments or our title, but if we are to lay down our lives, we must get our eyes off ourselves and what we deserve and instead place our eyes on the One who demonstrated pure, selfless love for us.

Forgiveness is a part of laying down our lives. It really means laying down our right to hold something over another person. When we hold on to past hurts or pains in an attitude of unforgiveness we are not laying down our lives for others. I know it is difficult to forgive and may even seem impossible. It sometimes seems more comfortable to hold on to that hurt or pain instead of letting it go. But letting go is also a picture of sacrificial love.

Jesus showed us this love on the cross when He said, "Father, forgive them, for they do not know what they are doing."[10] We have been forgiven of all our sin, and so we too must forgive others. We have no right to hold anything over another person. Go to the One who is the great forgiver and seek His help in forgiving others. Brennan Manning wrote, "God's glory is to forgive...It is effortless for God to forgive. God delights in forgiveness, because his forgiveness generates new life in us."[11]

Forgiving doesn't mean you allow someone to walk all over you again and again. In fact you may need to set some healthy boundaries as you recognize someone's potential to hurt again. Forgiveness may take time—time to work through the pain, to grieve the loss of what could have been—but we must move forward and let go. It's not an easy process, but it is a freeing one. As has been well said, "Forgiveness does not change the past, but it does enlarge the future."[12]

If you feel as though you can't forgive, I would encourage you to first go in quiet and solitude to your heavenly Father and seek His help. You may also want to visit with a biblical counselor or godly trusted friend to help you walk through the tough journey of forgiveness. It is a high calling of obedience. Because Jesus laid down His life to provide forgiveness for us, we ought to lay down what we perceive as our rights in order to walk in forgiveness and sacrificial love for others.

To be sure, not everyone is easy to love. As much as we would enjoy being surrounded by kind, refreshing, and uplifting people throughout our lives, the reality is that we are going to encounter some difficult people along our journey. Whether co-workers, family members, neighbors, or others, there are certain people who can suck us dry emotionally. Others demand our time and attention physically. Certainly, we must be understanding and gracious, realizing that difficult people have typically had a bit of a rough past or may be going through something challenging in their personal lives. As we seek to love sacrificially, we may also need to learn to set some healthy boundaries, as I mentioned earlier.

In her book *Setting Boundaries with Difficult People,* my friend Allison Bottke writes, "It's our responsibility (and no one else's) to understand our identity and define our personal boundaries, to identify where we start and end and where the other person starts." She goes on to say, "If you're struggling with difficult people, the problem probably has to do with absent, misdrawn, or poorly defined boundaries—yours or theirs."[13] We must carefully consider how we can sacrificially love with strength and wisdom, while also deliberately determining where we must draw the line to maintain peace of mind.

As we step back and take in the beauty of the picture John has painted for us of the love Jesus demonstrated, we are motivated and inspired to reflect His love toward others. Laying down our lives for others builds bridges and deepens relationships. When we cling to our rights and live for ourselves, we build walls of stone around our hearts. Ask God for direction in how to love like He has with the people around you in your daily life. Let's continue to think about what John said that sacrificial love looks like in a practical sense.

Practicing Love

If we are to love like Jesus did, by laying down our lives for our brothers and sisters, then what does that look like in my day-to-day living? John provides a practical picture of selfless love:

1 JOHN 3:17-18

If anyone has material possessions and sees a brother or sister

in need but has no pity on them, how can the love of God be in
that person? Dear children, let us not love with words or speech
but with actions and in truth.

Jon Katov felt as though he was "doing his duty" by joining his church group once a month to hand out energy bars near a homeless shelter in Phoenix, Arizona. Jon's view of sacrificial love was forever changed when he met Steve. Jon was surprised how easy the man was to talk to, but he was even more surprised when Steve asked if he could go and visit the church where all these nice people attended who had come to help the homeless. *Um…well…okay,* Jon thought to himself. *This was supposed to be a nice, safe trip to hand out energy bars to the homeless. This wasn't supposed to go beyond taking a little of my time on a Saturday morning. Now this is getting personal.*

Jon agreed to pick Steve up and take him to church the next Sunday—and yes, the homeless man looked a little different than the clean and well-fed people in Jon's congregation. But Steve and Jon began visiting and talking, and Jon began to realize that his acquaintance was a normal person who had experienced some hard times and bad breaks in life. Jon also recognized that although he himself had a network of people to help him if he needed advice or assistance, someone like Steve had no one. Jon began to dream about what it would look like if a group of people surrounded Steve and helped him get back on his feet again.

Jon asked his friend what his goals and dreams were. Simply put, Steve wanted to have a place to live and to become a security guard one day. Jon put together a group of caring and sensible people, whom he referred to as "The Table" because they came around the table and served as a type of board of directors for Steve, meeting together with him and helping him reach some of his goals. They made legal and medical connections and helped Steve make it to his first interview.

Now, Steve is no longer homeless but is sustaining himself. Yes, it took extra time and effort on Jon's part—more than he bargained for when he set out to hand out energy bars—but he made a difference in one man's life.

Now Jon has gone on to help others with this same concept of reaching out and building relationships with the homeless. His organization, called Open Table, arranges for 12 people to surround and help a homeless person who is ready to get out of poverty. It is effective, and it is working, but it demands one thing: sacrificial love. Jon saw a need and didn't turn his head the other way—he reached out and made a difference.*

Let's go further than simply our words or good intentions! Let's be willing to step out of our comfort zones and reach into the lives of others. Jon did it by going the extra mile in Steve's life, which eventually led to the start of the Open Table movement. What gifts or abilities has God given you to share? Open your eyes to the needs God has put in front of you and take a step forward in selflessly loving your brothers and sisters.

> *Father, shine Your love brightly through us. May our love for our brothers and sisters reflect the love You have for us. Help our love to be sincere as we demonstrate compassion to others in need.*

Heart Confidence

Love. Sacrificial love. The beautiful evidence of God within our hearts is expressed in the bright and brilliant shades of sincere and genuine love toward others. But perhaps you are like me, always thinking I could do more. I tend to compare myself with Jon Katov; or with Karen, who goes out every Saturday and brings breakfast to families in need; or with Jewel, who lovingly and tirelessly brings the gospel to women in Nigeria and Peru and wherever else God opens the door. That little tug in my heart says, *You are not doing enough. If you really loved Jesus you would do more.*

We must be careful of comparisons and recognize that God has given each of us different responsibilities. In painting the picture of

---

* You can find out more about Open Table at their website: www.theOpenTable.org.

what true love looks like, John ran the risk of his readers becoming legalistic or dogmatic about the principles of love. We are tempted to beat ourselves up for not doing as much as we should or could. The apostle wanted to make sure we didn't jump into the performance-track mentality, which takes our eyes off the Lord. Gently and lovingly John continues his masterpiece of love by reassuring believers that we can set our hearts at rest in God's presence:

1 JOHN 3:19-24

This is how we know that we belong to the truth and how we set our hearts at rest in his presence: If our hearts condemn us, we know that God is greater than our hearts, and he knows everything. Dear friends, if our hearts do not condemn us, we have confidence before God and receive from him anything we ask, because we keep his commands and do what pleases him. And this is his command: to believe in the name of his Son, Jesus Christ, and to love one another as he commanded us. The one who keeps God's commands lives in him, and he in them. And this is how we know that he lives in us: We know it by the Spirit he gave us.

In all honesty, how could we ever do all that we can to love others in this world? It's impossible! There will always be one more mouth to feed, one more heart to touch, one more need to meet. As true followers of Christ, His Spirit within us moves us to love and reach out to others, but only Christ Himself loved perfectly. We fall short. There are many times when we fail to meet a need, many times when we do not sacrificially love. It may be tempting to begin questioning whether we are really a Christian because we are so aware of our shortcomings in giving love. I'm thankful that John addressed the fact that we are not perfect. He knew our hearts would condemn us, so he strengthens us with the truth that God is greater than our hearts. He knows everything.

God knows our hearts, and He knows if we have placed our faith in Christ. It is not our love or our works that save us or allow us to be considered clean in God's sight. It is rather His love for us, displayed in what Jesus did on the cross, that saves us. Paul's letter to the Romans reminds us that for this reason there is no condemnation for those who are in Christ Jesus, those who have placed their trust in Him.

Most likely John was reflecting on the words of Jesus that he recorded in his Gospel:

> *If you remain in me and my words remain in you, ask whatever you wish, and it will be done for you. This is to my Father's glory, that you bear much fruit, showing yourselves to be my disciples.*
>
> *As the Father has loved me, so have I loved you. Now remain in my love. If you keep my commands, you will remain in my love, just as I have kept my Father's commands and remain in his love. I have told you this so that my joy may be in you and that your joy may be complete. My command is this: Love each other as I have loved you.*[14]

There is great joy as we abide in God's love and reflect that love to one another. As we love the Lord with all our heart and genuinely love His people, we can also have confidence in our prayer life. Prayer is not a game of "If I do this, I will get that." Prayer is a joining with God in doing His work. It means approaching our heavenly Father with a desire to love Him completely and a desire to love our brothers and sisters in a sincere way. When we bring these desires before God, we can come to Him confidently knowing He will answer them.

John's engaging portrait of love has the artist's signature theme throughout his work—it is the beauty of abiding in Christ and He in us. Although John has mentioned several times the importance of remaining in Christ, this is the first time we see a reference to the Holy Spirit in his letter. We know that we are in Christ "by the Spirit He gave us." I like what John Owen said: "The Holy Spirit is the great beautifier of souls." Isn't it amazing and wonderful that our kind Father has given us His Spirit to dwell within us? We are not alone—we have the privilege and honor of God Himself dwelling in us. Oh, how valuable we are to Him, for He has given us His Spirit!

God's Spirit not only helps us to genuinely love others, He also comforts us in our affliction, prays for us when we do not have the words to utter, gently convicts us of sin, and guides us along the right path. What confidence we have in knowing God's Spirit abides in us and works through us! We do not have a distant relationship with God—rather, we have an intimate and heart-to-heart relationship with Him that comes when we open the door to His Spirit through placing our faith in Christ.

My friend, have you experienced that deep and abiding relationship with God? Are you aware of His presence in your life? John Calvin wrote, "As the soul does not live idly in the body, but gives motion and vigor to every member and part, so the Spirit of God cannot dwell in us without manifesting himself by the outward effects."[15] When God's Spirit governs our lives, we will be recognized as His children, for the evidence of love will be unmistakable. Lest we become prideful of how we sacrificially show love and compassion to our brothers and sisters, let us always remember that it is His Spirit at work within us.

In John's portrait of love we see the vibrant colors of the Trinity: the gracious love poured out in us from the Father, the genuine love demonstrated to us by Jesus, and the evidence of the Holy Spirit as He lives and loves through us. It's a complete picture! As we step back and observe John's picture of love, we see that it illustrates God, for God is love. If we need to know what love looks like, we need look no further than to Him. And if we need help in loving others, we know the source of love. If our hearts are hungry for love, in Christ alone we find fulfillment.

Thank You, Father, for loving us so completely. Help us to show the world what Your love looks like.

One of my favorite songs we sang in the chapel choir was "Joyful, Joyful, We Adore Thee," set to the tune of the "Ode to Joy" in Beethoven's Ninth Symphony. I still sing it in my heart to this day. The words illustrate the beauty of God's love reflected in this world:

> Joyful, joyful, we adore Thee,
>   God of glory, Lord of love;
> Hearts unfold like flow'rs before Thee,
>   op'ning to the sun above.
> Melt the clouds of sin and sadness;
>   drive the dark of doubt away;
> Giver of immortal gladness,
>   fill us with the light of day!
>
> Mortals, join the happy chorus,
>   which the morning stars began;
> Father love is reigning o'er us,
>   brother love binds man to man.
> Ever singing, march we onward,
>   victors in the midst of strife,
> Joyful music leads us Sunward
>   in the triumph song of life.[16]

Getting Personal

ABIDING TRUTHS:

- Guard your heart against hatred.
- Look to Christ for a perfect picture of love.
- Be willing to lay down your life in the form of serving others.
- Open your eyes to the needs of your brothers and sisters.
- Prayer is partnering with God in His work.
- We can pray with confidence as we live in Him.

- Because we are believers in Christ, God has given us His Holy Spirit.

ADDITIONAL READING: Romans 5 and 8

ACTION STEPS: Opening our hearts

It is my hope that this chapter inspired you to love in actions and not just words. I hope it ignited a desire in your heart to open your heart and reach out to a brother or sister in need. This begins with prayer and wisdom from above. Ask God to open your eyes to the needs around you and show you how to demonstrate His love toward others through selfless acts of kindness and service. Take a step out of your comfort zone in the days and weeks ahead and actively put your love into action. Perhaps it is bringing dinner to someone who is bedridden, helping someone with their garden, visiting someone in a nursing home, or taking food to the local food pantry. In the space provided below write down how you demonstrated God's love "with actions and in truth."

on't Be Fooled

*"False teaching not only poisons the mind,
but also demoralizes the life."*

GEOFFREY B. WILSON

*"We have received, not the spirit of the world,
but the Spirit who is from God,
that we might know the things that have
been freely given to us by God."*

1 CORINTHIANS 2:12 NKJV

As a single woman, Meagan had become discouraged by the dating scene and began to wonder if she would ever meet Mr. Right. But when David was hired by her firm she began to see a glimmer of hope in her otherwise bleak-looking list of prospects. She felt a bit of giddiness inside her when he invited her to join him for lunch. As they visited over a hamburger, she found herself drawn to his piercing blue eyes and casual way of viewing life. He was not only handsome, he was also smart, athletic, and hardworking—and most important, he said he was a Christian. After a few delightful lunches they began to officially date each other. They had so much in common—sports, work, travel, and many other hobbies and interests. The pair quickly became enamored of one another to the point where they spent most of their time together.

They talked about religion a little bit, at least enough to know that they both had an interest in spiritual things. Since they both went to church it was no surprise when David invited Meagan to join him at his church one Sunday. When she inquired about what type of church it was, David replied it was called the Church of Divine Light. He explained that since religion seems to separate people, his church embraced a variety of concepts, including Christianity. Meagan thought that sounded pretty good and, of course, very loving.

The preacher at the Church of Divine Light delivered an eloquent sermon. His message seemed to loosely tie in with some things Meagan remembered from Sunday school as a kid. Now she wished she was a little more knowledgeable about the Bible because she wasn't so sure about all the things that David's church seemed to believe. She listened intently as the preacher passionately declared: "Man is saved by knowledge and by believing in the Teacher, God, and by being baptized for the forgiveness of sins. Thus, he receives knowledge and strength to be able to obey the law."[1] He went on to say, "This salvation has nothing to do with the redemption of every human soul. It is a grand, cosmic process. It is the return of all things to their state before a flaw in the realm of the good brought matter into existence and entrapped some of the divine light. The spirit of the Christ was sent as a savior who united himself with Jesus, the son of Mary, at His baptism."

Meagan's head was spinning. *This man talks about Jesus and seems to have spiritual insight, but I've never heard this stuff before. I don't even understand what he is saying.* After church, David and Meagan went to lunch. "I thought you said you were a Christian," she burst out. He smoothly replied, "I said I believed the Christian faith, but I don't think Christians control the marketplace on spiritual ideas. I embrace a variety of different concepts concerning divine inspiration and the man Jesus."

Meagan didn't know a lot about what the Bible had to say, but she did know that her Christianity was built on believing that Jesus is the Christ, the Son of God, and so she decided that was probably the next question to ask. "What do you believe about Jesus?" she inquired. David pondered the question for a minute and then reflected on some sermons he'd heard from his preacher. "Well, Jesus was certainly a good man, but he never claimed to be divine. He had the spirit of the Christ descend on him at some point, which later then left him. You see, I believe our universe is made up of two realms, the good and the evil. The spirit of the Christ rules over the good and he is given the world to come. The Prince of evil is the prince of the world. The spirit of the Christ is between God and creation—he is not a creature, but still not comparable or equal to God."

Hmm…Meagan was going to need to think about this. It was all so confusing. David sort of seemed to accept some of her Christian beliefs. Why should she let a few little differences drive a wedge into their wonderful, almost perfect relationship? Didn't God say that we are supposed to love everyone anyway? Meagan's hunger for love drew her to David as she rationalized that she was demonstrating love and graciousness toward her friend in accepting the fact that he had a slightly different belief system than she did. Instead of studying what the Bible had to say about the deity of Jesus and its teaching that Jesus Christ is God in the flesh, Meagan slowly gravitated toward David's religion, as it seemed new and fresh and exciting to her.

She was giving her heart to David rather than to the One who is love and could fulfill her longing for love. Ironically, the message she heard was actually quite similar to the old false teachings that circulated in John's day. There is truly nothing new under the sun!

Like Meagan, many people today are slowly led astray by false teachings and man's self-contrived spirituality. When we are not rooted in God's Word, the strong current of philosophies or even partial truths about Jesus can carry us away with fine-sounding arguments. It is easy for those who do not know the Bible to be confused and deceived by ideas that have just a little truth mixed in them. As we study John's letter together we learn that he had a pressing concern about those who taught half-truths about Jesus. He warned,

1 JOHN 4:1-3

Dear friends, do not believe every spirit, but test the spirits to see whether they are from God, because many false prophets have gone out into the world. This is how you can recognize the Spirit of God: Every spirit that acknowledges that Jesus Christ has come in the flesh is from God, but every spirit that does not acknowledge Jesus is not from God. This is the spirit of the antichrist, which you have heard is coming and even now is already in the world.

Spiritual Examination

John told the early believers to test the spirits to see whether they are from God. Don't believe every spiritual idea that comes down the pike or every popular concept that appears in the latest bestseller. Examine the claims—do they line up with Scripture? Do they just sound good because they have a few Bible verses thrown in there, or do their words align with the truth of the Bible? Paul, in his first letter to Timothy, warned, "The Holy Spirit tells us clearly that in the last times some will turn away from the true faith; they will follow deceptive spirits and teachings that come from demons. These people are hypocrites and liars, and their consciences are dead."[2]

Paul went on to challenge Timothy, "Focus on reading the Scriptures to the church, encouraging the believers, and teaching them."[3] Paul knew that as we examine the Scriptures and know what the Bible says, we are able to recognize deceptive teachings. Just like Paul, John warned that in the last days there will be many false prophets, those who claim to have a message from God, but they do not speak the truth about Christ. Be diligent to examine the Scriptures and know what they have to say about Him. Jesus is Truth. Let us love the Truth with our whole hearts.

As has been often pointed out, when the FBI trains their agents to recognize phony money, they do not have them study the counterfeit; they have them study the true money. We too should study Christ in order to recognize false teachings about Him. John said that one of the most important tests for false teachers is this: Do they acknowledge that Jesus Christ came in the flesh? When we listen to a teacher or preacher or read a supposedly Christian book we must always consider, Who do they say Jesus is? Do they acknowledge that Jesus is God incarnate (God in the flesh)?

Bottom line, Jesus is all God and all man. The Bible reminds us that "in Christ all the fullness of the Deity lives in bodily form."[4] John was greatly concerned about the wave of ideas that seemed to be flowing through the culture and leading astray those who did not have a full understanding of Christ. When we look at his Gospel we see that John reveals why he wrote this important account of Jesus' life:

> *Jesus performed many other signs in the presence of his disciples, which are not recorded in this book. But these are written that you may believe that Jesus is the Messiah, the Son of God, and that by believing you may have life in his name.*[5]

Matthew, Mark, and Luke were all written before John penned his Gospel. John could have sat back in his elderly years (as mentioned earlier, it is thought that he was around 90 years old when he wrote his Gospel) and rested from all his life work and teaching, yet he felt compelled to write his perspective. He added incidents and accounts that are not shared in the other Gospels. He wrote with one theme in mind, that people would know that Jesus is the Messiah, the Son of God. Let's take a look at some of the ways John portrayed his beloved Savior.

Jesus from John's Point of View

In his Gospel, John wanted his readers to know who Jesus Christ was, and so he included the significant statements Christ made about Himself. He included seven "I AM" statements that Jesus made identifying Himself as the Messiah, the Son of God. Let's take a look at each one:

1. The Bread of life.

> *Jesus declared, "I am the bread of life. Whoever comes to me*

will never go hungry, and whoever believes in me will never be thirsty."[6]

Bread satisfies our physical hunger just as Jesus satisfies our spiritual hunger. Although with physical bread we will hunger again, with Christ we are spiritually satisfied and will never be in need of anything else but Him. In the Old Testament, God provided manna from heaven to meet the Israelites' needs, and God has provided the Bread of Life to meet our need for redemption, love, and the forgiveness of our sins.

2. The Light of the world.

When Jesus spoke again to the people, he said, "I am the light of the world. Whoever follows me will never walk in darkness, but will have the light of life."[7]

Notice that in 1 John we read that "God is light," and here we see Jesus proclaiming that He is the Light of the world. Those who follow Christ are no longer in darkness, but those who reject Christ live in darkness. He brings the light of salvation, the warmth of love, and the brightness of truth to our lives. In the Old Testament God provided a pillar of fire to light the way for the Israelites through the wilderness to the Promised Land; in Jesus, He has provided the one true Light that lights our way to salvation. As His Spirit dwells within us, we too are lights. Jesus told us to let our lights so shine that others may see our good works and honor the Father.

3. The Gate.

Jesus said again, "Very truly I tell you, I am the gate for the sheep. All who have come before me are thieves and robbers, but the sheep have not listened to them. I am the gate; whoever enters through me will be saved. They will come in and go out, and find pasture."[8]

Jesus is the sole entrance to the Father. He clearly is identifying Himself as the way (the gate, the door) to God. Just as a shepherd would lie down across the entrance to the sheep pen, acting as the gate, so Jesus laid down His life, providing the way of salvation. There is no greater love than offering your life for another.

4. The good Shepherd.

> *"I am the good shepherd. The good shepherd lays down his life for the sheep. The hired hand is not the shepherd and does not own the sheep. So when he sees the wolf coming, he abandons the sheep and runs away. Then the wolf attacks the flock and scatters it. The man runs away because he is a hired hand and cares nothing for the sheep. I am the good shepherd; I know my sheep and my sheep know me."*[9]

By declaring Himself the good Shepherd, Jesus is saying that He is both *good*, and He is a *shepherd* for His sheep. A hired hand is not necessarily a good shepherd (perhaps referring to the religious leaders of His day). We read in Luke that Jesus said, "No one is good—except God alone." So by calling Himself *good* He is equating Himself with God. As a shepherd, Jesus lovingly cares for us and tends to our needs. What an amazing thought that we are His sheep and under His care!

5. The Resurrection and the Life.

> *Jesus said to her [Martha], "I am the resurrection and the life. The one who believes in me will live, even though they die."*[10]

This is a powerful statement. Jesus claimed to be both the Resurrection and the Life. Who can provide eternal life? If Jesus were a mere man, then He would have been deluded to say that He could provide both resurrection and life. Yet as God in human form, He had every right to proclaim what He alone could provide. No one else can make such a claim to have power over life and death except for God Himself.

6. The Way, the Truth, and the Life.

> Jesus answered, "I am the way and the truth and the life. No one comes to the Father except through me."[11]

Here, Jesus is responding to Thomas, who wants to know the way to heaven and to God. Jesus provided one of the clearest replies we can find in Scripture—*He* is the way to God, the truth of God, and the provider of life. There is no other. God in His loving-kindness provided a way for sinful man to have eternal life with Him in heaven. Jesus said the Way is found in Him, the Truth is found in Him, and Life is found in Him.

7. The true Vine.

> "I am the true vine, and my Father is the gardener...I am the vine; you are the branches. If you remain in me and I in you, you will bear much fruit; apart from me you can do nothing."[12]

Not only does Jesus provide the Way to salvation, but He also offers us a way to have a fruitful and meaningful life. Through this metaphor of the vine and the branches, Jesus taught the basic essential of Christian living. We are not alone trying to make sense of life without His help—rather, we are connected to the One who gives us strength, hope, and nourishment. We are to abide (dwell, remain) in Him and He in us, so we will bear much fruit—for without Him we can do nothing. A fruitful life is one filled with purpose—it brings beauty and nourishment to this world. How wonderful to know that He loves us so much He wants us to constantly abide together with Him!

Christ also performed many miraculous signs demonstrating His deity and His power over nature. John included seven of these "signs" in his Gospel. Remember, John's purpose was to show and convince the reader of Jesus' true identity as the Son of God, both God and man.

These signs proved that Jesus was in fact God because of His supernatural display of power, which pointed to deeper divine realities. Let's take a glance at them and consider what they reveal about Jesus.

1. *Turning the water into wine.* [13] Jesus' first miracle proved His deity through His ability to create something from nothing. Think about it this way too—this miracle showed His power over time as well, since wine needed to be aged. Jesus created the best wine, and He created it right there and then. (Just a little side note: If God instantly created good wine that had every characteristic of having been aged, what can that tell us about the creation of the universe?)

2. *The healing of the royal official's son.* [14] Jesus demonstrated His deity in His power over space and distance when He healed the official's son without actually being in his presence. God's power is not limited to location. He is ruler over all time and space.

3. *The healing of the lame man.* [15] Jesus healed this man on the Sabbath, which caused quite a stir among the religious leaders. He used this miracle to show that He is Lord of the Sabbath, and to teach that He is one with His Father. In this miracle we see Jesus' clear indication that His own deity is one with God. Jesus said, "Very truly I tell you, the Son can do nothing by himself; he can do only what he sees his Father doing, because whatever the Father does the Son also does."

4. *The feeding of the multitude.* [16] This sign, in which Jesus takes a little boy's lunch of two fish and five loaves of bread and feeds over 5000 people, demonstrates His power over the natural or created world. Isn't it interesting that the two signs showing Jesus' power over creation (changing water into wine and the feeding of the crowd) had to do with the elements of the last supper—the wine and the bread?

5. *Walking on water.*[17] Jesus walked on the water to join His disciples in their boat. As soon as He got into the boat, it immediately was at the shore. Here we clearly see His power over the laws of nature. God's power has no boundaries, no limits. He is not ruled by the laws of nature, for He rules over all creation.

6. *The healing of the blind man.*[18] John shares the delightful story of Jesus healing a man who was born blind. It is one of my favorite stories in the Bible, and actually has a humorous element. You can read the whole story in John 9. In this sign we see His power to re-create eyes that can see. Not only did Jesus demonstrate His power over physical blindness, but He also used this as an opportunity to show that He can heal spiritual blindness. He said, "For judgment I have come into this world, so that the blind will see and those who see will become blind."

7. *The raising of Lazarus.*[19] Certainly this is one of Jesus' most dramatic displays of power—He raised a man to life who had clearly been dead for several days. Here we see Jesus' power over life and death. If no other miracle portrayed Jesus as the Christ, this one did without a doubt. Many believed on Him that day, although the religious leaders continued to be blind with envy.

As you can see, Jesus not only described His deity in a variety of ways, He also demonstrated it through His actions and power. What will you do with the truth you know about Jesus? As for me, when I consider the truth about who Christ is, I must fall on my knees and confess that Jesus Christ is Lord. I am compelled to love Him more deeply and follow Him more sincerely. I am grateful for the beauty of His love for me, and I am forever thankful for His sacrifice on the cross on my behalf. I can confidently cast my cares on Him, for He is not only able to meet my needs, but He also lovingly cares about my life. What will you do with this Jesus?[20]

Spiritually Smart

Do you ever wish you had listened a little better in your high-school history class? The other day Curt and I watched a documentary on World War I, and I could hardly remember how the war began. I must admit that I was so distracted in high school, thinking about boys or who was popular or what I was wearing, that I didn't listen or hold on to facts that didn't seem important to me My grades were pretty good despite my shallow interest, but now I'm slightly embarrassed that I don't seem to know important facts about history I should have learned. I guess we tend to remember what is important to us, and old wars couldn't compete with prom and homecoming.

What we choose to listen to spiritually makes a difference in how we live our lives and interact with other people. We must be discerning. When it comes to spiritual matters, there are many voices out there, but not all of them are from God. We learned in our passage earlier in this chapter that we can distinguish between those whose message is for Christ and those whose message is against Him. The one who acknowledges that Jesus is the Christ, the Son of God, is from God. Now John makes a distinction between what the world listens to and what Christ's followers listen to for direction and truth in their lives:

I JOHN 4:4-6

You, dear children, are from God and have overcome them, because the one who is in you is greater than the one who is in the world. They are from the world and therefore speak from the viewpoint of the world, and the world listens to them. We are from God, and whoever knows God listens to us; but whoever is not from God does not listen to us. This is how we recognize the Spirit of truth and the spirit of falsehood.

In today's culture there is no shortage of voices that speak from the viewpoint of the world. The world perks up and listens to those who speak with a world-centered point of view. But we, as followers of Christ, have a different way of listening, and our ears ought to be tuned into the truth. There are two different ways to look at our circumstances: We can look at them from an earthly perspective, or we can look at them from a Christ-centered perspective. Once again John is helping us understand that as Christians we are different. We have the Spirit of God within us. John has already warned us not to be surprised if the world hates us, and now he is pointing out that we have completely different perspectives.

The apostle Paul also wrote about the different way the world views things. In Ephesians we read,

> *I tell you this, and insist on it in the Lord, that you must no longer live as the Gentiles do, in the futility of their thinking. They are darkened in their understanding and separated from the life of God because of the ignorance that is in them due to the hardening of their hearts. Having lost all sensitivity, they have given themselves over to sensuality so as to indulge in every kind of impurity, and they are full of greed.* [21]

To the Romans Paul wrote,

> *Although they knew God, they neither glorified him as God nor gave thanks to him, but their thinking became futile and their foolish hearts were darkened. Although they claimed to be wise, they became fools and exchanged the glory of the immortal God for images made to look like a mortal human being and birds and animals and reptiles.*
>
> *Therefore God gave them over in the sinful desires of their hearts to sexual impurity for the degrading of their bodies with one another. They exchanged the truth about God for a lie, and worshiped and served created things rather than the Creator— who is forever praised.* [22]

We do not want to become futile in our thinking. We do not want to exchange the truth about God for a lie. So how do we tell the difference between a world-centered viewpoint and a Christ-centered one? Here are some basic differences and distinctions between the two:

World-centered	*Christ-centered*
Morality is relative. I can live how I think best.	God's ways are best and I want to please Him.
We evolved—life is random.	We were created; God has a purpose for us.
Things and people can satisfy.	God's love is generous, compassionate, and fulfilling.
Man is basically good.	Man is sinful and needs a savior.
Jesus was a good man.	Jesus was the Son of God who came to be the Savior of the world.
There are many ways to God.	Christ is the only way.
Christ, plus our works, brings salvation.	Faith in Christ only is the way of salvation.

As you can see, there are no small differences between the world's point of view and a viewpoint that is centered on Christ. It makes a difference which point of view you choose to adhere to. John didn't want the early believers to be distracted by false teachings or enamored by the viewpoints of the world. Instead he drew the line to make sure they listened to the truth.

What about you—what voice is your ear attentive to? Let us turn our ears to listen to the voice of love and truth and build our lives on the sure foundation of Christ and His Word. We must know the Word and listen to it. May I encourage you to be diligent to not only read it daily, but to study it and know its truth, so that you will not be distracted by the interests of this world. Ask God to help you to listen to His truth and understand what it says.

We are reminded of one marvelous truth in this passage that gives us hope and strength in our daily lives. Did you find the golden nugget of wisdom within John's words here? For those who are believers in Christ, he writes, "The one who is in you is greater than the one who is in the world." Oh, the glorious power in that statement of faith! We are not alone. We have the Spirit of the living God dwelling in us to help us listen to His voice, discern His truth, and overcome the false teachings centered on the world's point of view. His Spirit within us keeps our eyes looking upward toward the One who is above every power and authority. His Spirit comforts us through troubles and constantly reminds us of the Father's unfailing love. The One who is in us is greater than the one who is in the world!

Getting Personal

ABIDING TRUTH:

- Be careful of those who want to lead you astray.

- Test every spirit to see if it is from God.

- We must study Jesus in order to recognize faulty philosophies and ideas about Him.

- All the fullness of God dwelt in Jesus in bodily form.

- John wrote his Gospel to help people know the truth and believe.

- Listen to the voice of truth.

- The One who is in you is greater than the one who is in the world.

ADDITIONAL READING: 2 John

ACTION STEPS: Spiritually smart

Take some time to review each of the signs Jesus performed.

Beside each one, write something you learn about Jesus that you can take to heart. How does each truth affect you personally?

1. Turning the water into wine (John 2:1-11): _____

   _____

2. The healing of the royal official's son (4:46-54): ____

   _____

3. The healing of the lame man (5:1-23): _____

   _____

4. The feeding of the multitude (6:1-15): _____

   _____

5. Walking on water (6:16-21): _____

   _____

6. The healing of the blind man (9:1-41): _____

   _____

7. The raising of Lazarus (11:1-57): _____

   _____

What is the most significant way Jesus has made a difference in your life? _____

_____
_____
_____
_____
_____

PART FIVE

Loving Because We Are Loved

"O love of God, how strong and true!
Eternal and yet ever new;
Uncomprehended and unbought,
Beyond all knowledge and all thought."

HORATIUS BONAR

"I will praise you, LORD, among the nations;
I will sing of you among the peoples.
For great is your love, higher than the heavens;
your faithfulness reaches to the skies.
Be exalted, O God, above the heavens;
let your glory be over all the earth."

PSALM 108:3-5

CHAPTER NINE

Organic Love

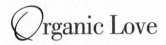

*"I know of no truth in the whole Bible
that ought to come home to us with such power
and tenderness as that of the love of God."*

D.L. MOODY

*"God demonstrates his own love for us in this:
While we were still sinners, Christ died for us."*

ROMANS 5:8

Eleven-year-old Anjit would hardly look up into the face of the man who had just handed him 50 rupees. He quickly stuffed the generous gift (equivalent to about two US dollars, about half-a-month's wages for laborers in India) into his pocket as he continued creeping along from train car to train car, wiping the floor with an old shirt. Ben knew that Americans were discouraged from handing out money to the Dalits and beggars, but he just couldn't help it when he saw this pitiful boy, hungry and helpless, just trying to survive. Ben and his team weren't even supposed to be on this particular train headed from Hyderabad, India, to a small town about five hours away. They had been scheduled to travel on a much nicer train that didn't allow beggars in the passenger cars, yet a train strike had forced them to take whatever train they could.

As Anjit made another pass through the car, one of the members of Ben's group, who spoke the local language, began to engage the boy in conversation. Although they invited Anjit to sit with them on the bench, he refused, knowing that he would be beaten by the police if he were seen taking a spot on the train. Anjit's story was not much different from many of the Dalits (more commonly known as *untouchables*, the lowest of the caste system—or recently as *slumdogs*, from the movie *Slumdog Millionaire*). He scavenged whatever he could in order to eat and survive. His father was an alcoholic and continually stole what little money his son earned, using it for liquor and leaving his family to starve.

Anjit revealed he was running away from his father and was headed to a temple in order to offer a sacrifice of his hair, the only thing of value he had, in hope of finding help and a better life. It was then that the love of God broke through, as the men began to share the truth about Christ. Anjit understood the gospel and placed his faith in Jesus. The missionary continued to tell him about Christ's love and how Christians do not need to make sacrifices at a temple to a god, since the Son of God made the ultimate sacrifice for us. The men encouraged Anjit and prayed with him.

One of the men in the group was wearing a cross he had made from nails and hung around his neck on a leather strap. Anjit took an interest in it, so the man immediately gave him the cross. The boy gladly received it. Interestingly, Anjit never got off the floor, and even after the men had finished visiting with him, he humbly scooted off that train car and into the next, accompanied by the derision of the other passengers. The men never expected to see him again and didn't even know where he got off the train.

Ben's team spent several hours at their destination, at a dedication for a church in the village. When it was time to return to Hyderabad they barely caught the train, literally running to jump on it as it pulled out of the station. This time they had the opportunity to sit in one of the more comfortable front cars where no beggars were allowed. One of the men was headed to the back of the car to the restroom, when he noticed a young boy waving at him from the car behind. He didn't recognize him at first, but when he held up the cross from around his neck he knew immediately it was Anjit!

The reunion was sweet. They were completely amazed they had ended up on the same train once again, since Anjit's destination city was two hours east of Hyderabad. The entire team encircled the boy to visit with him. They couldn't believe the transformation in the young man in appearance and demeanor, all in just the few short hours they had been apart.

Anjit told them he had used the money Ben had given him to get a haircut and bath. He had also been able to buy some new clothes and a ticket for the train to take him to a place where he knew he could find a job. He was a new person and gladly told everyone he saw, "I'm a Christian! I'm a Christian!" The men wrote down the information about where he was headed so they could try to stay in touch with him and encourage him in his new journey.

One of the men in the group was able to follow up with the young man and helped connect him to a Bridge of Hope program hosted by Gospel for Asia.[1] There Anjit learned English and was cared for by loving workers. He was equipped with skills to find a job, as well as with the wonderful truth of God's love. Isn't it amazing how God can use one simple act of compassion to transform a life and make a difference in this world?

True Love

True love is not passive or stagnant—rather, it is vibrant, flowing, and active. True love looks for opportunities to reach out and touch another's life. True love changes lives. How do we understand what pure and organic love looks like? Where do we go to find a definition or explanation of true love?

Think of it this way: If I am wondering how a word is defined, I look it up in a dictionary. If I want to know about an event in history, I look it up on the Internet. If I want to know how to cook a brisket,

I look up the recipe in a cookbook. When I want to know what love is, I look at God. He defines love. He demonstrates love. He portrays love in its purest and richest sense. The greatest portrait of love this world has ever known is drawn for us by our heavenly Father. His very nature is love.

The closer we grow to God, the more His love is reflected in our lives. Just as the moon reflects the brilliant light of the sun, so those who love Christ reflect His love to others. On its own, the moon is simply a dusty gray ball, but when it reflects the light of the sun it shines with brilliance and strength. Now the Bible doesn't call us moons, but it does call us clay pots. We may not have the capacity to love with a sincere and selfless love in our own strength, but as we know the love of the Father through Christ, His love shines brightly through us. Without Christ, we do not have the capacity to show *agape* love.

I'm reminded of what Paul wrote to the Corinthians: "God, who said, 'Let light shine out of darkness,' made his light shine in our hearts to give us the light of the knowledge of God's glory displayed in the face of Christ. But we have this treasure in jars of clay to show that this all-surpassing power is from God and not from us."[2] How do we love more richly and deeply? We look to the One who defines love. We receive His love. We experience it. We live it and breathe it. Oh, what beautiful women we are when we reflect the love of the Father because we know Christ and walk closely with Him, adoring Him, and fellowshipping with Him.

John, the beloved disciple, enjoyed a close fellowship with Christ. He reflected Christ's love because he spent much time with Him. As John returns to the topic of love in his letter, we come to one of the most oft-quoted passages in Scripture:

1 JOHN 4:7-8

Dear friends, let us love one another, for love comes from God.
Everyone who loves has been born of God and knows God.
Whoever does not love does not know God, because God is love.

Since love is intrinsic to the nature of God, a deep and abiding relationship with Him will produce love in our lives. Now, sadly, I must add that this verse has been used and abused in a myriad of ways. Some have misused this verse to say that anyone and everyone who has love in their heart, no matter what they believe, knows God and is His child. We must be careful to take this verse in context and with the whole of Scripture. As we saw earlier, John is writing this book specifically to believers in Christ. In his Gospel, the apostle writes that those who have received Christ have the right to be called children of God. It is only through Christ that we can sacrificially love others.

In the 1960s (I was just a wee little child back then, of course) I remember that the love movement was the "in thing." People had T-shirts and bumper stickers with big flowers that said "Love Power" or "Make Love, not War." I remember hearing about lovefests or "love-ins," which as a young girl I didn't quite understand. Love became supreme in this movement. Instead of glorifying God, who embodies love, people glorified love, making *it* into their god. Of course this shallow 1960s version of love was founded on the notions "If it feels good, do it" and "All you need is love." The love that people seemed to make into their god (along with sex and drugs) became unfulfilling and dissatisfying.

We must be clear—love isn't God. The truth of the Scripture is that God is love. Love is the essence of His being and is exemplified in all He does. When we concentrate on the rich truth of these verses our lives can be transformed. Think of it! We as believers in Christ have the overwhelming joy of having a relationship with the God whose very nature is pure love in its truest and most organic sense. I am at a complete loss to try to describe the wonder and joy I feel right now as I think about His love and the fact that He is the lover of my soul. All we need is love indeed—and God is love.

His love is unsearchable, unthinkable, unfathomable, unimaginable. It is boundless, endless, grace-filled, all-encompassing. His love is unshakable, unmovable, immeasurable. We cannot wrap our minds around the fact that a perfect God would love us. Only through His Spirit can we even begin to comprehend and embrace how wide and long and high and deep is the love of Christ. Every action God does is done out of love. Every word He speaks is born out of love.

Haven't we all at some point in our lives desperately tried to find someone who will love us completely? We hope for it, we long for it, we dream of it like a princess in a fairy tale. And yet no one—no husband, no parents, no kids can demonstrate the truest of love, which can only be found in God. Our search for that abiding love ends at the cross. It is there we find the fulfillment we are seeking. It is in Christ alone that we know true love. When we finally realize and embrace His grace-filled love, we ourselves become satisfied, filled up, and overflowing with it. When we are spilling over with His love, it can't help but pour out to those around us.

Fulfilling Love

Born in 1648, Jeanne Marie Bouvier de la Motte's family was among the aristocracy of France. Although as a youth she was religiously inclined, when Jeanne grew into a young lady she became rather vain and proud, and as a social butterfly she gave very little thought to God. Her family gave her hand in marriage to Monsieur Jacques Guyon, who was at least 20 years her senior. She soon discovered that her married life would be a difficult one because her mother-in-law (who lived with them) ruled the home with a rod of iron. During these painful years as a young bride Jeanne felt as though she lived in what she called "a house of mourning." Yet God used this time to draw her back to Himself. Through much affliction, Jeanne's faith in a loving God grew richer and deeper.

Madame Guyon's life was riddled with heartache as she not only endured her less-than-perfect marriage, but also the deaths of her beloved son, her father, and her stepsister. Although each of these brought pain, they also served to broaden her love of the Savior. At a time when the church viewed a relationship with God as a religious and formal observance, Madame Jeanne Guyon wrote about a personal relationship with Him and the intimacy of His love. Because of her beliefs and her writings she was imprisoned for much of the latter period of her life. When she died at the age of 69 she had penned over 60 volumes. Many of what are considered her sweetest poems and most insightful books were written during her imprisonment.

Her passion and love for God have influenced a number of great preachers and teachers throughout the ages. Despite her difficult life, she thrived on the nourishment of God's rich love for her and His presence in her life. Her prayer life was deep and satisfying; she dwelt on God's presence in her life and beheld His great love for her. Here is a reflection from one of her writings about dwelling on Christ and turning to Him in faith:

> So that you can see him more clearly, let me describe the way in which you come to the Lord by the simple act of beholding him and waiting upon him. You begin by setting aside a time to be with the Lord. When you do come to him, come quietly. Turn your heart to the presence of God. How is this done? This, too, is quite simple. You turn to him by faith. By faith you believe you have come into the presence of God.[3]

When we are still and reflect on the beauty of God's magnificent love for us, our hearts are transformed, and we see life in a different way. When we trust His love, we know that no matter what happens to us, we are cared for by a loving God. We cannot know the reason why He allows certain trials to enter our lives, but He who did not spare His only Son understands our heartache and loves us in whatever place we are. Let us not think that if we're going through a difficulty that He must not love us. He doesn't demonstrate His love by giving us a nice and easy life. No, God showed His love for us through a much more meaningful sign.

In 1747 Charles Wesley penned the words of a beautiful hymn that reflects God's divine love. Here are some of the verses:

> Love divine, all loves excelling,
>   joy of Heav'n to earth come down;
> Fix in us Thy humble dwelling;
>   all Thy faithful mercies crown.
> Jesus, Thou art all compassion,
>   pure unbounded love Thou art;
> Visit us with Thy salvation;
>   enter every trembling heart.

Breathe, O breathe Thy loving Spirit,
　　into every troubled breast!
Let us all in Thee inherit,
　　let us find the promised rest;
Take away our bent to sinning;
　　Alpha and Omega be;
End of faith, as its beginning,
　　set our hearts at liberty.

Come, Almighty to deliver,
　　let us all Thy grace receive,
Suddenly return, and never,
　　never more Thy temples leave.
Thee we would be always blessing,
　　serve Thee as Thy hosts above,
Pray, and praise Thee without ceasing,
　　glory in Thy perfect love.

What passion this hymn instills in the hearts of those who have received His love! May we reflect the love we have so lavishly been given. Not that we loved God, but that He loved us and sent His one and only Son to pay the price for our salvation. This kind of love spills over from our lives into the lives of others. We are vessels of divine love pouring out His message of love to a love-thirsty world. Here's how John portrayed it:

1 JOHN 4:9-12

This is how God showed his love among us: He sent his one and only Son into the world that we might live through him. This is love: not that we loved God, but that he loved us and sent his Son as an atoning sacrifice for our sins. Dear friends, since God so loved us, we also ought to love one another. No one has ever seen God; but if we love one another, God lives in us and his love is made complete in us.

We need look no further than the cross to be reassured of God's love for us. We always have this one fact to reflect upon. May we never lose our first love, the joy we feel when we first recognize what God has done for us. I like to reflect upon this demonstration of love every single day, and as I do I am always overwhelmed and strengthened by the fact that the great God of all creation offered His Son on our behalf. In turn, I am compelled to reflect such a great love to my brothers and sisters in Christ. John said that the sign that God's love lives in us is if we love one another. Have you noticed he repeated this one truth over and over again? Perhaps he was continually reflecting on Jesus' words— "By this everyone will know that you are my disciples, if you love one another."[4]

Confident Love

My husband was a wild man in high school. We won't go into how he lived or what he did, but suffice to say, he was running *from* God, not *to* Him. On Christmas break during his senior year he was invited to attend a church retreat. Curt didn't have anything better to do, and he thought there might be some cute girls on the trip, so he agreed to go along. Each night when the group would gather to hear a message from the Bible, he had no interest at all and usually just skipped out on the sessions. But one night for some reason he decided to stay and listen.

The story of God's love demonstrated on the cross became very real to him. He had always thought that if you become a Christian and then mess up, you step out of God's grace and are no longer saved. But this night the pastor talked about the fact that once you trust Christ you are sealed until the day of redemption. This shined a whole new light on Curt's dark view of Christianity. The pastor taught from a passage in Ephesians, which says, "You also were included in Christ when you heard the message of truth, the gospel of your salvation. When you believed, you were marked in him with a seal, the promised Holy Spirit, who is a deposit guaranteeing our inheritance until the redemption of those who are God's possession—to the praise of his glory."[5]

That was it! That was the "aha!" moment for Curt, when he realized he could place his faith in Christ and that God's Spirit would come into his life. The Spirit would not only help him live for Christ, but He was also the seal of guarantee that he would be God's child until the day of redemption. It was that very day that Curt placed his faith in Christ and what Christ did for him on the cross. There was a dramatic change in his life. He began living for Christ and getting to know what the Bible had to say about Him. God began to turn him from a man who lived life on his own terms to a man who desired to serve God.

When we place our faith in Christ we can be confident of His unfailing love. He allows us the privilege of having His Spirit dwell within us. We do not need to live in fear and trembling, hoping He will accept us on the day of redemption. No, we can trust His love and redemption for *everyone* who trusts in Christ. John wrote about this confidence we have in God. Interestingly, with John having lived in Ephesus, we can see the same truth written in Paul's letter to the Ephesians (which we read earlier in this section) in the following passage by John:

1 JOHN 4:13-18

This is how we know that we live in him and he in us: He has given us of his Spirit. And we have seen and testify that the Father has sent his Son to be the Savior of the world. If anyone acknowledges that Jesus is the Son of God, God lives in them and they in God. And so we know and rely on the love God has for us.

God is love. Whoever lives in love lives in God, and God in them. This is how love is made complete among us so that we will have confidence on the day of judgment: In this world we are like Jesus. There is no fear in love. But perfect love drives out fear, because fear has to do with punishment. The one who fears is not made perfect in love.

John reminded believers of the confidence they can have in Christ on the day of judgment. Those who have placed their faith in Christ have no need for fear because perfect love drives out fear. Now, I only know of one perfect love and that is the love God has for us—the love

He demonstrated for us on the cross. This is the love that clears away our fears. Because of His perfect love we can live without fear before God. We who acknowledge that Jesus is the Son of God have God's Spirit living in us and do not live in fear, knowing we are sealed to the day of redemption. What confidence we have, not in ourselves, but rather in His perfect love! Did you catch what John wrote? "And so we know and rely on the love God has for us." We don't rely on ourselves, but we rely on His trustworthy love.

Motivation to Love

Throughout our lives we tend to be motivated in different areas and by a variety of stimuli. For instance, when I go to my closet and my favorite pair of jeans doesn't fit anymore, then I'm motivated to get a little more serious about diet and exercise. When I can't seem to find the ingredients for a recipe in my cluttered spice cabinet, then I'm motivated to reorganize all those little bottles. When Curt tells me he thought the dinner I prepared was delicious, I'm motivated to cook that meal again.

As humans, we often work best by motivation. That's how God made us. When it comes to loving and forgiving others, we may need a little motivation as well. Let's face it, it's not always easy to love other people, especially the annoying ones who complain nonstop or the gossips who have hurt our feelings. Why love them? The reason is simple. We love because while we were yet sinners, God showed us love. We have been forgiven of all our sins, and so we too must forgive others. God has lavished His love upon us to the point that we are motivated to sincerely love others. John wrote about this motivation:

1 JOHN 4:19-21

We love because he first loved us. Whoever claims to love God yet hates a brother or sister is a liar. For whoever does not love their brother and sister, whom they have seen, cannot love God, whom they have not seen. And he has given us this command: Anyone who loves God must also love their brother and sister.

We are inspired to love sacrificially because we are loved in this manner. Let us spend quiet moments like Madame Guyon did, reflecting on the wonder and magnificence of His love. As our hearts are filled with gratitude for the love God has for us, then we overflow with love toward others. But we must be drinking it in on a regular basis. When is the last time you stopped and simply reflected on His love? May I encourage you to take some time, even a moment right now. Put down this book, close your eyes, and reflect upon the fact that you are sincerely loved. Think on the cross and thank the Lord for placing His Spirit within you. Ponder the fact that the God of all creation has allowed you to have His Spirit.

Allow your heart and mind to be filled with the joy of His love and His presence in your life. Keep in mind that hatred for our brothers and sisters and love for God cannot exist together. Like oil and water, they just don't mix. In this passage we not only understand our motivation to love, we also are told it is a command. John doesn't just leave it up to us if we feel like it. We are commanded to love. Let us not love in only the words that come out of our mouths, but through the deeds we do each day.

Laundry Love

When's the last time you were motivated to do someone else's laundry? I'm barely motivated to do my own laundry, much less anyone else's. Several years ago a life group from a church in California decided to ask the question, "What can we do?" They sincerely wanted to demonstrate God's love in a tangible way to those who live in poverty in their local community. So they decided to collect their quarters and some laundry soap, went down to the Laundromat, and offered to pay for people's laundry and help with the folding. Their effort turned into a movement called Laundry Love. Now there are more than 40 Laundry Loves started in the United States.

Cleaning the clothes and bedding of those in need offers dignity, health, hygiene, and hope. It's about more than just the clothes; it's about the relationships. Those living in shelters or who are homeless begin to feel as though someone cares and that they are worthy of love.

It's a modern-day "washing of the feet," if you will. It began with one act of kindness, reaching out to touch someone who needed to see a hint of God's love and care, and it grew into a national initiative of compassion.*

Demonstrating God's love is not always convenient or comfortable. It means stepping out of our orderly lives and reaching out to lift up another person. Yet isn't that exactly what Jesus did for us when He left the orderliness and perfection of heaven and came to this earth to offer His life for us? If you are struggling with how to reach out to another, ask our loving heavenly Father to guide you and lead you in how you can show His love in a tangible way. He's an expert in the area of love!

Getting Personal

ABIDING TRUTHS:

- Love is intrinsic to the nature of God.
- We learn what love looks like by looking to Him.
- His love transforms us into people who love.
- His love is indefinable.
- Those who have trusted Christ do not need to fear on the day of judgment.
- Love for God and hatred for our brothers and sisters cannot co-exist.
- We are commanded to love our brothers and sisters.
- Our motivation to love is the fact that we are loved first by God.

ADDITIONAL READING: Ephesians 1

---

* You can go to www.Just4one.org to learn more and get involved.

ACTION STEPS: Never forget

Our motivation to love others stems from knowing how completely loved we are by the Father. It is easy to become distracted from our first love. In Revelation we read that Jesus had this warning for the church at Ephesus: "I hold this against you: You have forsaken the love you had at first. Consider how far you have fallen! Repent and do the things you did at first."[6] So we must ask ourselves, do we love God with the same fervor we did when we first followed Christ? How do we return to that first love? If we heed Jesus' words, we repent, which means to stop and turn back to Him. We can do the things we did when we first understood God's love for us. When we fall in love we act differently. There is a joy and excitement in our newfound love. We spend time together. Let's fall in love with Jesus all over again!

How would you describe your love for God when you first believed and followed Christ? _____

_____

_____

_____

How would you describe your love for Him right now?

_____

_____

_____

How can you return to your first love of Christ?_____

_____

_____

_____

CHAPTER TEN

God's Family Portrait

"'What shall I do, then,
with Jesus who is called the Christ?'
This is the most important question
that has ever been asked.
It is also the question you must ask yourself."
BILLY GRAHAM

"The Spirit Himself testifies with
our spirit that we are children of God,
and if children, heirs also, heirs of God
and fellow heirs with Christ,
if indeed we suffer with Him so that we
may also be glorified with Him."
ROMANS 8:16-17 NASB

When my dad turned 65 years old we decided to do a family portrait with all the kids and grandkids. As you can imagine it was quite a challenge to pull together 14 active people with busy schedules, yet between the soccer games and piano recitals we were able to make it happen. More than a decade later, we still look at that picture with fond memories, as it is a reflection of love of family as well as perseverance and strength. You see, after the tragic and sudden death of my mother, who was hit and killed by a car when she was only 55 years old, my sister, dad, and I had walked the road of grief and sadness together. Dad remarried several years later after meeting a godly and compassionate woman named Janet.

Admittedly, spending holidays together as a blended family was not easy at first. The two sets of relatives hardly knew each other, and we weren't sure we really liked each other, but one thing kept pulling us together, and that was the common bond of our parents. And we are different. Wait a minute, let me rephrase that—we are complete opposites. My stepsister Stacey typically refers to herself as "Mrs. Negative," and I'm known as the "Positive Lady." Yet despite our different personalities and viewpoints we have grown together as a family. We may not understand each other completely or agree on every detail, but we have learned to appreciate our differences and build on the common bond we have.

If we focused on our petty differences, we would experience unpleasant family gatherings. Since I love my dad, I want to love his family. Now I want you to know that my dad is not a domineering or demanding father. He doesn't hold a long list of rules and regulations over us children. His desire is simply that we love each other. Our family portrait, although different from what I thought it would be, is a picture of loving each other because of our common bond.

∽

John wants the family of Christ to have a loving family portrait as well. Our loving heavenly Father tells us to love His Son, first and foremost. He also tells us to love each other as brothers and sisters in Christ. We have a unique bond. Our common bond is our faith in Christ. The world may not understand us. Some may try to require more from us, but God's commands for us are simple and clear: Believe in His Son and love each other. John continually revisited the basic principles of Christianity to make sure believers understood clearly what it meant to be a part of God's family. He wrote,

1 JOHN 5:1-5

Everyone who believes that Jesus is the Christ is born of God,
and everyone who loves the father loves his child as well. This is
how we know that we love the children of God: by loving God
and carrying out his commands. In fact, this is love for God:
to keep his commands. And his commands are not burdensome,
for everyone born of God overcomes the world. This is the vic-
tory that has overcome the world, even our faith. Who is it that
overcomes the world? Only the one who believes that Jesus is
the Son of God.

What are our Father's desires? John mentioned them earlier in his letter, "This is his command: to believe in the name of his Son, Jesus Christ, and to love one another as he commanded us."[1] To believe in the name of Jesus Christ means we place our faith in Jesus (*Yeshua*— the One who will save His people) Christ (*Messiah*, the Anointed One sent by God). Faith in Christ and love for our brothers and sisters in Christ are God's commands. Faith and love go hand in hand. Our faith in Christ plays out in a love for Him and a love for His people.

Once again John reminded believers that God's commands are not burdensome. I'm sure he constantly thought about Jesus' words—"My yoke is easy and my burden is light."[2] The Pharisees tried to weigh down God's people with needless and burdensome rules and regulations. Yet Jesus said all the commandments basically come down to this: Love God with your entire being and love others as you do yourself. A world-centered point of view says, "Faith in Christ is not enough. You must do more, work harder, and live in constant guilt."

Imagine the burden I would feel if I thought I had to constantly perform for my dad in order to prove I am part of his family. "Dad, in order to prove that I'm your child I went to your office today and cleaned the floors and the bathrooms." Or "Dad, in order to earn my right to be your daughter I have gone on 12 mission trips in foreign countries." Or "Dad, in order to make sure I'm your child I have volunteered one day a week serving the homeless." Now I'm not saying we shouldn't do sacrificial acts of service—obviously that is what a large portion of this book is about. I'm simply saying that they do not earn us the right to be called God's children. The works we do are a demonstration of our faith and love, but they are not what makes us a part of His family. John asked and answered that question: "Who is it that overcomes the world? Only the one who believes that Jesus is the Son of God."

Many religions today are built on doing works instead of trusting in faith to gain salvation or a right relationship with God. Even some popular Christian pastors and books tell us (in creative ways) that we are not doing enough and we must do more in order to really be saved. Be careful! Do not replace the cross of Christ with your own performance. Listen to John's words—"His commands are not burdensome." The world focuses on works; God focuses on faith. John wrote, "Everyone born of God overcomes the world. This is the victory that has overcome the world, even our faith." It is our faith in Christ that saves us. It is our faith in Christ that binds us together in Christian love. It is our faith in Christ that gives us victory over sin and death.

Victorious Followers

There are many wonderful descriptions used throughout Scripture to speak of the followers of Christ. Words like *sheep, branches, saints, witnesses, redeemed* all are accurate portrayals, but John emphasizes a glorious and unique point. We are *victorious* over the world. John uses several different variations of the word *overcomer* to describe Christ's followers. In fact, of the 24 times the word is used in the New Testament, John uses it in his writings 21 times. We saw it earlier in 1 John 4:4: "You, dear children, are from God and have overcome them, because the one who is in you is greater than the one who is in the world."

What a tremendously uplifting statement! As God's children, we are victorious because we have the Spirit of the living God dwelling within us. We need not live in fear of the spirit of this world (the enemy or those who oppose Christ), for God's Spirit is greater than the spirit that is in this world. The Greek word for *overcome* is *nikao*, meaning "to conquer," "to overcome," or "to be victorious." It implies superiority over opposition. Jesus used this term in reference to Himself in conversation with His disciples, saying, "These things I have spoken to you, so that in Me you may have peace. In the world you have tribulation, but take courage; I have overcome the world."[3]

Being victorious doesn't mean the road will be easy for believers. The word itself implies that we have overcome something, that there is a battle or a struggle. As believers we can sense this struggle daily as we feel the tug of the world's desires or the temptation to worry or despair. Yet through these struggles, it is our faith that gives us victory, our faith in the all-powerful God whose Spirit is present in our lives. The apostle Paul reminded us to "take up the shield of faith, with which you can extinguish all the flaming arrows of the evil one."[4]

Isn't this the message of John and of the cross? Rejoice in the victory of what Christ did. We are overcomers because of what He did, not what we have done ourselves. Because of our faith in Him and our love for Him, we naturally want to live in obedience to Him. Victory over sin doesn't mean we will never sin again, but it does mean the penalty for our sins has been nailed to the cross. It also means that we have the Spirit of the living God dwelling in us, giving us the power to overcome the temptations in our lives.

In Romans we see this same theme of overcoming:

> What, then, shall we say in response to these things? If God is for us, who can be against us? He who did not spare his own Son, but gave him up for us all—how will he not also, along with him, graciously give us all things? Who will bring any charge against those whom God has chosen? It is God who justifies. Who then is the one who condemns? No one. Christ Jesus who died—more than that, who was raised to life—is at the right hand of God and is also interceding for us. Who shall separate us from the love of Christ? Shall trouble or hardship or persecution or famine or nakedness or danger or sword? As it is written:

"For your sake we face death all day long;
we are considered as sheep to be slaughtered."

No, in all these things we are more than conquerors through
him who loved us. For I am convinced that neither death nor
life, neither angels nor demons, neither the present nor the fu-
ture, nor any powers, neither height nor depth, nor anything
else in all creation, will be able to separate us from the love of
God that is in Christ Jesus our Lord.[5]

Nothing can separate us from the love of Christ. Because of Christ, the vast divide between holy God and sinful man has been overcome, and nothing can separate us from His love.

We are overcomers in many other areas of life as well. Our faith in a sovereign God allows us to have victory over fear and despair. When we face troubles or setbacks, our faith in a good and loving God encourages us and enables us to walk through our grief and step forward in His plan for our lives. Faith in an all-present God gives us strength to carry on, recognizing we are not alone. Yes, we are more than conquerors because of our faith in Christ Jesus!

Paul wrote to the Colossians about the spiritual triumph we have in Christ:

When you were dead in your sins and in the uncircumcision
of your flesh, God made you alive with Christ. He forgave us
all our sins, having canceled the charge of our legal indebted-
ness, which stood against us and condemned us; he has taken it
away, nailing it to the cross. And having disarmed the powers
and authorities, he made a public spectacle of them, triumph-
ing over them by the cross.[6]

Yes, Jesus triumphed over the powers and authorities of this world (both physical and spiritual) by the cross. The cross represents victory to us. When you wear a cross, wear it with great joy and confidence, for it is a symbol that the One who died on that cross and dwells within us has overcome the world.

Can I Get a Witness?

In the justice system, an eyewitness account has a powerful effect on the verdict. A study conducted in 1979 revealed a 54 percent swing from a not-guilty to guilty verdict within a case simply through the introduction of an eyewitness.[7] The power of a witness is significant, and because of that potential it is vital that the witness be reliable and trustworthy. A credible witness is not one who is speaking hearsay or reporting what they thought they saw. Factors for determining the credibility of eyewitness testimony in United States court systems include the following:

- The witness had personal knowledge.
- He or she was actually present at the scene.
- The witness paid attention at the scene.
- He or she told the whole truth.

It is not the number of witnesses that matters in determining credibility. The question for the jury is not which side has the most witnesses, but rather which witnesses' testimony they believe. Bottom line: Only the quality or power of believability matters.[8] Now if God Himself testified in a court of law, I'm pretty sure the jury would believe Him. He would be on the top of my list for credibility—how about yours? Yes, the God of truth is trustworthy indeed.

When it comes to identifying who is the Christ, the Son of God, I would take God's testimony over anyone else's. He is without a doubt a credible witness:

- He has personal knowledge of His Son.
- He has been present on the scene for eternity.
- He pays close attention, for He knows and sees everything.

- He does not lie. He speaks only the truth.

Without a doubt, I would say that God's credibility is far above and beyond that of any human witness. Those who proclaim, "Well, if God would just come down and tell us who the Christ is, or the way to be saved, then I'd believe and follow Him." News flash—God did tell us! The most credible witness in all the universe has testified about Christ.

Just as people in John's day questioned Jesus' divinity, so we still have those who question today. John addressed the truth by pointing out the credibility of the witnesses:

I JOHN 5:6-10

This is the one who came by water and blood—Jesus Christ. He did not come by water only, but by water and blood. And it is the Spirit who testifies, because the Spirit is the truth. For there are three that testify: the Spirit, the water and the blood; and the three are in agreement. We accept human testimony, but God's testimony is greater because it is the testimony of God, which he has given about his Son. Whoever believes in the Son of God accepts this testimony. Whoever does not believe God has made him out to be a liar, because they have not believed the testimony God has given about his Son.

The Old Testament law required the testimony of two or three witnesses to establish truth. Let's explore the three witnesses that John cites in his letter: the Spirit, the water, and the blood.

The *Spirit of God* boldly testified on the day Jesus was baptized. We read the account in Matthew's Gospel: "As soon as Jesus was baptized, he went up out of the water. At that moment heaven was opened, and he saw the Spirit of God descending like a dove and alighting on him. And a voice from heaven said, 'This is my Son, whom I love; with him I am well pleased.'"[9] At the Transfiguration with Peter, James, and John, God spoke in a similar fashion, "This is my Son, whom I have chosen; listen to him."[10] Yes, God's testimony was clear.

The Spirit of God also testifies in our hearts. He is the one who allows us to understand who Jesus Christ is and believe Him by faith. The Spirit comes to live in our lives, dwelling in us and transforming our lives. This too is His testimony.

John mentioned two other witnesses besides God's Spirit—the *water* and the *blood*. What in the world did John mean by that? Most likely the water referred to Jesus' baptism, and the blood referred to His death on the cross. We also know that John was standing there at the cross when the Roman soldier thrust his spear into Jesus' side and water and blood came pouring out. The poured-out blood and water were the physical credentials that Jesus was actually human and had most certainly died. This is significant because in order for Him to serve as our atoning sacrifice on the cross, He had to officially die. The water and the blood testify to the fact that Jesus did in fact die.

One other reason why John spoke of the water and the blood is that the false teachers asserted that the "Christ-spirit" descended on the man Jesus at His baptism (water) and departed from Him just before His death (blood). John declared Jesus' deity through both His baptism and His death. Interestingly, in the Old Testament the temple of the Lord was required to have a laver (water basin) for the washing of the hands as well as the sacrificial altar for the blood sacrifice. Both represent cleansing—the water cleanses the outside, representing holiness, while the blood represents being cleansed on the inside through the forgiveness of sins.

> *Father, thank You for the beauty of the water and the blood.*
> *Thank You for making us holy in Your sight, without blemish*
> *and free from accusation through Christ. Thank You for the*
> *testimony of Your Spirit. How wonderful that He dwells*
> *within us as a testimony and guarantee of Your salvation.*

The One and Only

Recently Curt and I enjoyed a short trip to Colorado with some friends. The cooler weather there is a welcome relief from the over-bearing summer heat in Texas. While we were there we decided to take a hike on a mountain path from one small town to another. It was a breathtaking, albeit challenging, journey over the mountains and through the woods, but it certainly offered magnificent photo opportunities. At one point on the journey there was a fork in the path. Arrows on the sign pointed one way to get to our destination village. It was a narrower, steeper path, but we knew it was the right way to where we wanted to go. The other path, the broader, easier one, was inviting, yet it eventually would have taken us back to where we started from, not where we were planning to go.

Now imagine if I had stood there at the choice of two paths and said, "I don't like this choice. I don't care if the arrows point to this smaller path as the right path—I want to go on the bigger, broader path. It looks like a much more fun and easy route. Besides, I'm sure all paths will lead to the town I want to go to and, beyond that, if I'm very sincere about my belief, it can lead me there. The person who made these signs is sooo narrow-minded!"

That's crazy! When the arrows provide information clearly showing me the correct path to my destination, I would be foolish not to believe it and go down that path. Yet how many people ignore the arrows pointing to Christ? How many claim it is narrow-minded to believe that the path God has provided is the only path to life for all who will believe and walk down it? John knew Christ personally. He was well aware that Jesus said He was the way, the truth, and the life. John's life was an arrow, pointing to the one and only way. There is one path that leads to life, John says, and everyone has received an invitation to walk down that path.

1 JOHN 5:11-12

And this is the testimony: God has given us eternal life, and this life is in his Son. Whoever has the Son has life; whoever does not have the Son of God does not have life.

John is drawing a clear arrow, don't you agree? There are no smudges on the sign or trees in front of it blocking our view of the direction it is pointing. It's clear; the person who has the Son has life. Those who choose to receive Him into their lives through faith experience abundant life here on earth as well as eternal life in heaven. Jesus said, "I am the gate; whoever enters through me will be saved. They will come in and go out, and find pasture. The thief comes only to steal and kill and destroy; I have come that they may have life, and have it to the full."[11]

Perhaps you are thinking, *What about the people in the deepest, darkest jungles somewhere who have not heard about Jesus?* I believe if God has provided a Way for salvation, He will also provide a way for all who are going to come to Him to hear about Him. He knows who will choose to follow Him.

Not long ago, I met a man from a small village who told the story of how someone happened to come to where he lived quite by accident and share the gospel. He said, "If anyone wonders how a person in the deepest, darkest jungle can learn about Christ, look at me. I am that man from a remote village in the deepest, darkest jungle, and God revealed Himself to me and now I live for Him."

Currently, there are many people who live in countries that are closed to Christianity. Amazingly, many reports are coming in from these countries about how Jesus has appeared to people in their dreams and they have come to faith in Him. I recently met a missionary from one of these countries, who shared with me a story of a man in a predominately Muslim country who was seeking the truth. For several nights Jesus appeared to him, showing him the way to salvation. To the amazement of the missionaries, this man understood the gospel and came to saving faith in Christ not through the missionaries' teachings, but through Christ making Himself known to him.

Author Lawrence Richards commented on this passage, saying,

> The claim that Jesus is the only way to God angered the people of the first century. They wanted to search for God in their own ways. They wanted their philosophies, their gods and goddesses who embodied human passions and reflected the image of man. Today too many people demand

the right to do their own thing in morals and religion. They reject the idea of an absolute. But John was not concerned with what people *want* to believe about God. John was concerned with *reality.* The fact is that God has spoken. *He* has said that only in Jesus can life be found. You or I may reject what He says, but our rejection will not change reality.[12]

The question is not, How will God take care of the people who haven't heard in the deepest, darkest jungles? We can trust the Almighty God to reveal Himself anywhere He chooses. The question is, What will we do with Jesus? Will we follow Him who gives us life, or will we reject Him and go our own way down our own path? Eternal life, abundant life is found in Jesus Christ. He is both Love and Life, and in Him we find fullness of joy. What would life be without the One who is life?

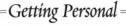

Getting Personal

ABIDING TRUTHS:

- God's commands are not burdensome.
- This is His command: Believe in His Son, Jesus Christ, and love each other.
- The world focuses on works—God focuses on faith.
- The victory that overcomes the world is our faith.
- The cross of Christ gives us victory over sin and death.
- Those who have the Son have life. Those who do not have the Son do not have life.

ADDITIONAL READING: Galatians 1 and 2

ACTION STEPS: Victory list

There is nothing more joyful than reflecting on who God is and the reality of His promises in His Word. Take some time today to consider the many ways you are an over-comer as a result of your faith in Christ. In this chapter I've already mentioned several areas in which we are overcom-ers (such as worry and sin), but now I want to encourage you to personalize the list. In what areas of your own life can you experience victory rather than discouragement or defeat? Fill in the blanks below.

Thank You, Father, that You are good and merciful. You are all-powerful, all-knowing, ever-present in my life. Because of my faith in Your abundant love for me, I have victory over…

_____

_____

_____

_____

_____

_____

_____

$\mathcal{K}$nowing We Are His

"Faith rests on the naked Word of God;
that Word believed gives full assurance."

H.A. IRONSIDE

"I thank my God every time I remember you.
In all my prayers for all of you, I always pray with joy
because of your partnership in the gospel from the first
day until now, being confident of this,
that he who began a good work in you will
carry it on to completion until the day of Christ Jesus."

PHILIPPIANS 1:3-6

CHAPTER ELEVEN

*U*tterly and Eternally Secure

*"A well-grounded assurance is always
attended by three fair handmaids:
love, humility and holy joy."*
THOMAS BROOKS

*"Now this is eternal life: that they know you,
the only true God,
and Jesus Christ, whom you have sent."*
JOHN 17:3

As a teacher and a speaker, my dad has often told the humorous story of the man who went mountain climbing by himself in the remote regions of the Sierra Nevada Mountains. As the experienced climber reached the top of one of the ridges he suddenly lost his balance and fell backward, but fortunately he had the presence of mind to grab a tree limb as he plummeted down the side of the mountain. As he hung on for dear life with his right hand, he cupped his left hand around his mouth and yelled toward the top, "Is there anyone up there? Can anyone hear me?"

After yelling in desperation for what seemed like an eternity he heard a powerful voice burst forth from the heavenly realm. The commanding voice said, "Do you trust me?"

"Yes!" cried the man in fear and desperation, "Yes, I trust you!"

The thunderous voice returned, "Do you trust me to help you?"

"Yes! Yes, I trust you will help me!" shouted the now exhausted and slightly impatient climber.

The heavenly voice responded, "Then let go of the branch!"

The climber considered the instructions and his options as he hung there in silence for a moment. Finally the climber got up enough courage to yell a weak response: "Is there anyone else up there?"

❧

There are some people who think that having faith in God is much like the experience of the poor, desperate climber hanging from a limb. Thankfully, as believers in Christ we can have confidence in God. Because of His great love for us, there are certain truths we can know about our eternal security and our relationship with Him. As John brought his letter to his fellow believers to a close, he reviewed the wonderful assurance they possessed in Christ. In the short passage we are going to explore in this chapter, John lists five certainties we can have as believers. He uses the word *know* as he introduces each of these truths. The Greek word he uses for *know* is *oida,* a perfect tense with a present meaning signifying "to have seen or perceived or realized." It implies a fullness of knowledge.

Here's what John identifies that we can know as believers. I call them the "We Know" statements:

1. We know we have eternal life.

2. We know we have what we ask if we ask according to God's will.

3. We know we have victory over sin.

4. We know we are children of God.

5. We know Jesus is the true God.

As His beloved children, we can live with a spiritual confidence. We can trust His promises for us and His great love toward us. He is faithful and true and will keep His promises. Let's go on a treasure hunt and discover the gems of assurance God has given us in His Word.

Assurance of Eternal Life

A number of years ago the sociology department of Baylor University (my alma mater) received a three-year grant from the John M. Templeton Foundation to conduct a nationally representative, multi-year study of religious values, practices, and behaviors. It included a selection of questions related to religious behaviors, beliefs, and belonging.[1] One question on the survey caught my eye especially in context of the passage we are examining in 1 John. The question was asked, "How certain are you that you will get into heaven?" Here are the responses:

2.5%—not at all certain

4.4%—not very certain

19.8%—somewhat certain

15.9%—quite certain

29.6%—very certain

11.4%—I don't believe in heaven

16.4%—I don't know

Let's consider the results. A little less than a third are "very certain" or seem to know they are going to heaven. A little over a third are what I would call "fairly certain"—hoping the odds lean in their favor, I guess. That leaves a final third, who really don't seem to know or care. Yet of the ones who are certain they are going to heaven, what do they believe is the key to spending eternity there?

In 2008, *USA Today* reported the results of a Pew research study, which revealed the variety of beliefs of those who call themselves Christians and what they believe about how to get to heaven. The survey found that many who identify themselves as Christians (29 percent) say they are saved by their good actions; 30 percent say salvation is through belief in Jesus, God, or a higher power; and 10 percent say salvation is found through a combination of behavior and belief.[2]

Wow! Not only is there a lot of confusion about whether we can know we are going to heaven, there also seems to be great confusion about how to get there! I'm thankful for God's Word, which gives us clarity and truth. Here's how John wrote about our confidence in having eternal life:

1 JOHN 5:13

I write these things to you who believe in the name of the Son of God so that you may know that you have eternal life.

Those who believe in the name of the Son of God, Jesus Christ, can know with all certainty that they have eternal life. Let us stand firmly, without faltering, on this truth. Paul wrote to the Colossians about "Christ in you, the hope of glory."[3] Yes, we can know that we have eternal life. The one who has the Son has life. The person who does not have the Son does not have life. How do you know that you have the Son? Believe on His name. That means trust that He is the Christ, the Son of God, the one who saves you. It is not your actions or your church attendance; it is placing your faith in Jesus as the one who paid the penalty for your sin.

Paul wrote, "It is by grace you have been saved, through faith—and this is not from yourselves, it is the gift of God—not by works, so that no one can boast. For we are God's handiwork, created in Christ Jesus to do good works, which God prepared in advance for us to do."[4] Clearly, God has good works that He has created us for us to do, but those good works are not what saves us. It is our faith. Good works and love for our brothers and sisters come as a result of trusting Christ. As we place our faith in Him, His love transforms our lives.

Thank You, Father, for the assurance You have given us of eternal life through faith in Your Son, Jesus.

Confidence in Prayer

My parents didn't give me everything I asked for—did yours? A wise and loving parent provides for the needs as well as some of the desires of their child, being careful not to overindulge them and create a self-centered monster. To tell you honestly, I'm so thankful God has not given me every little thing I asked for, because it would not have been in my best interest and not in accordance with His will. Many books have been written on how to pray effectively, but John addresses the matter of answered prayer quite succinctly here.

1 JOHN 5:14-15

This is the confidence we have in approaching God: that if we ask anything according to his will, he hears us. And if we know that he hears us—whatever we ask—we know that we have what we asked of him.

In our investigation of the "We Know" passages, John tells us how we can know that God hears us and that we will receive what we ask of Him: *If we ask anything according to His will.* Our life with God is a partnership, aligning our will with His and carrying out His work together. Our relationship with God is not a sugar-daddy relationship—if we want something, we ask for it and we get it. If you have ever observed parents spoiling their kids in this way, you have seen how unhealthy this type of relationship is.

Nor do we come before God as a fearful child, hoping He loves us and won't do us harm. No, we are reassured throughout Scripture that we can come boldly before the throne of grace, and that God invites us to ask, seek, and knock. Jesus said, "Which of you, if your son asks for bread, will give him a stone? Or if he asks for a fish, will give him a snake? If you, then, though you are evil, know how to give good gifts to your children, how much more will your Father in heaven give good gifts to those who ask him!"[5] May we be reassured that God is a kind heavenly Father who desires to give us good gifts!

Throughout his letter, John talks about remaining in Christ and abiding in Him. As we are working in relationship to God, not apart from Him, we seek His will. Our hearts are bent toward *His* desires for us, not *our* desires for us. Seeking His will means saying, "Father, I want what You want." How do we know what God wants? We begin in His Word. The Bible tells who He is, revealing both His nature and His will. Confession also allows us to pray according to His will because through confession we are agreeing with God that we have sinned and we need forgiveness.

David wrote,

> *Come and listen, all you who fear God,*
>> *and I will tell you what he did for me.*
> *For I cried out to him for help,*
>> *praising him as I spoke.*
> *If I had not confessed the sin in my heart,*
>> *the Lord would not have listened.*
> *But God did listen!*
>> *He paid attention to my prayer.*
> *Praise God, who did not ignore my prayer*
>> *or withdraw his unfailing love from me.*[6]

As we come to God we know we can pray in confidence as we pray according to His Word. Author Warren W. Wiersbe writes, "The most important thing about prayer is the will of God. We must take time to ascertain what God's will is in a matter, especially searching in the Bible for promises or principles that apply to our situation."[7] I'm always reminded of George Mueller, who would not even ask or pray for something until he found a promise in God's Word that he could literally put his finger on and claim. Mueller was a great man of faith whom God used in mighty ways. Let us come before God with reverence and love, seeking His will above our own desires.

Oh, the power of prevailing prayer! C.H. Spurgeon wrote, "If you would reach to something higher than ordinary groveling experience, look to the Rock that is higher than you, and gaze with the eye of faith through the window of importunate [persistent] prayer. When you open the window on your side, it will not be bolted on the other."[8] Let us go to the Father, our Rock, seeking His will and His way in our lives. I must admit, all too often I come to the Lord with my own personal agenda. As I examine John's words, I am personally challenged to lay my desires before the Lord and seek His will, not my own.

When we humbly come before the Father, let us begin by praising Him for who He is. As we praise Him for His sovereignty, we begin to recognize that His will is best, and it is what we want. Praying according to His will also means agreeing with Him that we are sinful and need Him. Often as I confess my sins and ask God to gently convict me of those sins I cannot or do not see, He changes my desires to coordinate with His. Let us be faithful to thank Him for His forgiveness through Jesus and thank Him for the specific work He is doing in our lives.

Thankfulness is an important part of praying in accordance with God's will. The psalmist wrote,

> *Make thankfulness your sacrifice to God,*
> *and keep the vows you made to the Most High.*
> *Then call on me when you are in trouble,*
> *and I will rescue you,*
> *and you will give me glory...*
> *But giving thanks is a sacrifice that truly honors me.*
> *If you keep to my path,*
> *I will reveal to you the salvation of God.*[9]

Earlier in his epistle John mentions the aspect of obedience to God's commands and the importance it plays in our prayer life. "Dear friends, if our hearts do not condemn us, we have confidence before God and receive from him anything we ask, because we keep his commands and do what pleases him."[10] Clearly, praying according to His will and walking in obedience go hand in hand. We must ask God's guidance and help as He gently reveals areas of disobedience in our own lives.

Now we come to an interesting part of John's letter, one that is much debated by theologians as to what specifically John is talking about:

I JOHN 5:16-17

If you see any brother or sister commit a sin that does not lead to death, you should pray and God will give them life. I refer to those whose sin does not lead to death. There is a sin that leads to death. I am not saying that you should pray about that. All wrongdoing is sin, and there is sin that does not lead to death.

I'll simply make a few comments. Many people wonder what the "sin that leads to death" is. And does John mean spiritual death or physical death? If he was referring to physical death, he perhaps could have been referring to the types of situations like the one Paul referred to in his first letter to the Corinthians. He said that some of them were taking communion in an unworthy manner, and for that reason some were sick and some had even died.[11] The sudden death of Ananias and Sapphira is another example of physical death due to sin: They were struck dead as a result of lying to God.[12]

It is possible that John is referring to spiritual death. Some commentaries refer to "blaspheming against the Holy Spirit," which we read about in Mark's Gospel.[13] Ultimately rejecting Christ leads to spiritual death, as we have already learned from John.

The early believers apparently would have known what John was referring to and so he did not elaborate on what this sin that leads to death is. The one thing we do know is that all unrighteousness is sin, and unless we put our faith in Christ, there are spiritual consequences of sin that lead to eternal death. Rest assured that if you have placed your faith in Christ you are sealed to the day of redemption.

Whether John is talking about physical death or spiritual death he was clear on the point that we ought to pray for a brother or sister who commits a sin. If we truly love our brothers and sisters, we do not want to see them sin. We need to help them, and we begin by praying for them. Paul wrote to the Galatians, "Brothers and sisters, if someone is caught in a sin, you who live by the Spirit should restore that person gently. But watch yourselves, or you also may be tempted. Carry each other's burdens, and in this way you will fulfill the law of Christ."[14]

When it comes to praying for our brothers and sisters who are wrestling with sin, doesn't that seem to be the last thing we tend to do? It is a sad truth that often Christians will gossip first and pray later (or not at all) in such a situation. Sometimes we may try to rush in and fix it or confront the brother or sister before we have prayed about it. John gives us a clear directive to pray for our brother or sister if we see them commit a sin. And I'm pretty sure John is not talking about sharing the request at a prayer circle. I believe he is talking about private prayer—just you and your heavenly Father.

We can pray for the one in sin to turn from it and abide in Christ. We can pray that God would lead us if we are supposed to confront them. We can pray that we guard our own hearts against judgment, gossip, or condemnation. Most important, we want to pray for our brother's or sister's continued spiritual growth.

We must leave the consequences of sin in God's hands, praying according to His will. Let us be faithful to pray for our brothers and sisters that they would walk in a manner worthy of their calling and that they would grow in the knowledge of God's will in all spiritual wisdom and understanding. One of the most loving things we can do is pray for the righteous walk and spiritual growth of our brothers and sisters. Even as I write this I realize that I'm not diligent enough in this kind of prevailing prayer for my sisters in Christ.

Victory over Sin

Several years ago a movie entitled *Taken* hit the big screen. It starred actor Liam Neeson playing the role of Bryan Mills, a retired CIA officer. Through a series of events, Bryan's 17-year-old daughter, Kim (played by Maggie Grace), was taken captive while on a trip to Paris with a friend. Her captors drugged her and sold her into a sex-trafficking ring. Of course they didn't realize they had messed with the wrong family. Bryan was immediately on the pursuit and finally hunted down and rescued his daughter from captivity in the sex-slave trade. Kim was powerless to rescue herself, but her dad had the firepower, the know-how, and the strength to find her and overcome her captors, setting her free.*

When someone is held captive in a situation like this, they are dependent on a rescuer. Spiritually speaking, we all need rescuing. The Bible says we have all been held captive by the power of sin and death, but those who believe in Christ have been rescued from the dominion of darkness and brought into God's kingdom. Our rescuer is Christ. Sin no longer has power over us, and it no longer dominates our life. As God's children we have power over sin because the One who is in us is greater than the one who is in the world. We may sin, but we have the power to choose not to continue in it. Sin doesn't control us; we have the Spirit of God giving us the ability to walk in a new direction.

John wrote about this power over sin in another "We Know" statement:

1 JOHN 5:18

We know that anyone born of God does not continue to sin; the One who was born of God keeps them safe, and the evil one cannot harm them.

We can walk confidently, knowing that our rescuer, Christ Jesus, keeps us safe and the evil one cannot harm us. We do not need to continue in sin. My friend, if you are struggling with an area of sin in your life, I want to encourage you first of all to identify it and recognize it as disobedience to God. Confess your sin to Him and seek His help to go in a new direction. I like what Oswald Chambers wrote: "When we realize that we have repeated a sin, the danger is to lie down in the mud and refuse to get up. There is no refuge in vowing or in praying; there is refuge in only one place, in absolute, childlike confidence in God."[15]

You may want to ask a sister in Christ to help you and hold you

---

* Sadly, sex trafficking is a reality in countries all over the world, and this movie brought to light the terrible plight of the young victims. Many groups are working tirelessly to help rescue those who have been sold through the system. International Justice Mission is one of those organizations of which I'm particularly impressed. International Justice Mission (IJM) is a human rights agency that brings rescue to victims of slavery, sexual exploitation, and other forms of violent oppression. You can visit their website at www.IJM.org to find out more information about their work.

accountable. You do not need to continue in sin, because God is more powerful than the enemy. Look to Him as your strength. Those who do not know Christ are powerless against sin, but believers in Christ are not powerless.

The Bible reminds us that our lives are hidden with Christ in God.[16] We are eternally safe in His arms—the enemy cannot snatch us away from the certainty that we are God's children. To be safe in God's arms doesn't mean that we will never face harm or difficulties or sadness in this world, but even here I'm reminded that the enemy can only operate within God's sovereignty. As we read in the book of Job, Satan was not able to go beyond what God allowed. Although we may not understand why God allows certain temptations, challenges, or even tragedies in our lives, we can trust His love, power, and sovereignty to work in ways beyond our understanding.

Children of God

The family of God and those who belong to the world are radically different. John tends to put things in an "either-or" type of way. Earlier in his letter we read his distinction that people are either children of God or children of Satan. He doesn't leave a lot of room for middle ground, does he? We either belong to the kingdom of God or we belong to the kingdom of this world. We come now to the fourth of John's five "We Know" statements:

I JOHN 5:19

We know that we are children of God, and that the whole world is under the control of the evil one.

Sadly, those who belong to the world are under the control of the evil one. People who don't know Christ are dominated by and are under the power and influence of the enemy. But you may say, "I know a lot of non-Christians and they are nice people. They aren't satanic or anything." We must look at what John is saying through spiritual lenses and see that because the world belongs to Satan, those who are of the world fall under his dominion. If I was born and raised in France, I may live in the countryside and never see the president of France, but I'm still a citizen of the country and fall under its rule.

On the other hand, if I have been adopted into a new kingdom I fall under the new kingdom's dominion and authority. We have been adopted into the kingdom of God. We are His children through faith in what Christ did for us on the cross. We have been changed and transformed into His children. Our Father has given us His Spirit to live in us as a seal and a promise that we are a part of His family. We can walk confidently, knowing we belong to Him.

As I write this it also makes me realize how much I don't want anyone to have to live under the dominion of the ruler of this world. I want everyone to know the joy of being a part of God's family. Let us be wise in the way we act toward outsiders (those who do not know Christ). May our conversation be full of grace, seasoned with salt, so that we may have an answer for anyone who asks us about the joy we have as one of God's children. Pray that God opens your eyes to those with whom you can share the wonderful news that there is hope in Christ, beyond the power of this world.

Jesus Is the True God

Ultimately it is God who gives understanding about Jesus Christ. He reveals the truth to those who will believe. Sometimes we get the feeling that someone's salvation rests in our hands and it is up to us to make them understand and believe, but John reminds us that it is God who provides that understanding. We must be faithful to share the wonderful truth of who Christ is, but God takes away spiritual blindness and allows people to see. People's salvation is not in our hands—it is in His hands. He gives salvation through Christ and brings people to salvation through the work of His Spirit, and it is a joyful blessing that we may have the opportunity to be a part of that process.

John's fifth "We Know" statement reminds us that it is God who reveals truth and leads us to the One who is true:

1 JOHN 5:20

We know also that the Son of God has come and has given us understanding, so that we may know him who is true. And we are in him who is true by being in his Son Jesus Christ. He is the true God and eternal life.

This word *true*—*alethinos*—means "genuine or sincere." John made his point over and over, making sure there was no room for doubt: Jesus is the real deal. He is the Christ, the anointed One, the Son of God, and through Him and Him alone we have eternal life. We can have complete certainty that Jesus Christ is the genuine and authentic Son of God. His incarnation is the seal and guarantee that confirms the other four "We Know" statements. Because of this "We Know," we can have confidence that the rest are valid!

John beautifully weaves God the Father and God the Son together in this verse. Jesus Christ came so that we may "know him who is true." And he continues by saying that "He is the true God and eternal life." A wonderful realization for us personally is highlighted in this verse as well: "We are in him who is true by being in his Son Jesus." What a high and joy-filled privilege to know that we are in Him! We have been brought to the Father through Christ, and we are a part of His family. We are in Him, and He is in us.

The glorious riches of this verse are that God the Father, God the Son, and God the Holy Spirit each represent "Him who is true." God three in one, eternal and true. They work as one and move as one. Jesus Christ, the Authentic and True One came in the flesh to offer His life for us and bring us to the Father. Those who believe in Him have the True One living inside them in the form of the Spirit. Have no doubt, fellow believers in Christ! We are secure in the True One, the One who provides eternal life. God is faithful! God is forever! God is true!

═══════════ *Getting Personal* ═══════════

ABIDING TRUTHS:

- We can be confident that we have eternal life through faith in Christ.

- We can be confident in prayer if we ask according to God's will.

- We ought to be diligent in praying for the spiritual strengthening of believers.

- We can experience victory over sin.

- We know we are children of God.

- We rejoice in knowing that Jesus is the true God.

- We have the One who is true and eternal dwelling within us.

ADDITIONAL READING: John 17

ACTION STEPS: Practicing prevailing prayer

As we learned in this chapter, we can pray confidently when we pray according to God's will. If you do not have an established time of prayer I would encourage you to determine a time and place each morning that you devote to God. If you already have a daily time of prayer, I encourage you to take it to a deeper level as you sincerely seek His will.

Begin with praising God and thanking Him. Take time to confess your sin and agree with Him that you need His help and are thankful for His forgiveness, mercy, and grace. Deliberately pray His promises. Keep your Bible open with you as you pray. Search the Scriptures for confirmation of His promises in His Word and put your finger on them as you pray. Acquiesce to His will, giving your desires to Him. Remember as you pray that you are partnering with Him in His work. Start a prayer journal to write down prayers for your spiritual strength and growth and that of other believers God has put in your life. As you spend this time in prayer, I know you will grow more deeply in love with Jesus, and His love will permeate your words and actions.

Chapter Twelve

First Place in Our Hearts

"We easily fall into idolatry,
for we are inclined to it by nature;
and coming to us by inheritance,
it seems pleasant."
Martin Luther

"My dear friends, flee from idolatry."
1 Corinthians 10:14

Once upon a time, in a land not too far from our own, a fair maiden named Gladis awaited her handsome prince. They were betrothed to be married in the coming year, yet until that time her beloved prince was away fighting battles and building the kingdom. Before he had left on his journey, he had reassured Gladis of his love and told her that if she needed anything while he was away she could confidently approach the king with her request. The king had promised to take care of her and freely give her all she needed as she prepared to one day live as the royal princess.

Gladis was thankful for all she had been promised, yet sometimes she became distracted by the delights in her small village. Her village was known for making jewelry—not real jewelry, only replicas of the beautiful genuine jewels in the king's possession. Gladis not only became enamored by the big, beautiful imitations of emeralds, sapphires, and rubies, she fell in love with the factory owner's son, named Gweed. Now, Gweed was nothing like the prince. The prince was strong and faithful and noble; Gweed was selfish and lazy and foolish. You may ask, How could Gladis fall in love with such a scoundrel when she has a wonderful prince who loves her?

It happened rather gradually. You see, while the prince was away, Gladis grew tired of studying her books on kingdom etiquette and preparing for her royal wedding. She no longer read the love notes her handsome prince sent her from his travels. Instead she began to wander around the village, and she always seemed to be drawn to the Glimmers Factory, owned by Gweed's father. There she examined the jewels and dreamed about what it would be like to have a crown full of them. She began trying on shiny rings and sparkling necklaces just to see what they would look like. Eventually Gweed started visiting with the fair Gladis as she frequented the factory, and soon they fell in love.

Although she had a handsome and wonderful prince awaiting her, Gladis wasted her days visiting with Gweed in meaningless conversation rather than preparing for her wedding. She spent her time playing with worthless gems instead of seeking real ones. Eventually her prince returned and came to take her to the kingdom, but Gladis was unprepared. She had fallen head over heels for Gweed and was so busy playing dress-up with gaudy fake jewelry that she completely forgot about her prince and the royal wedding. Silly Gladis!

⁂

Now if you are thinking that is the most ridiculous fairy tale you've ever heard, stop and consider that it is not so far-fetched. We are betrothed to the One True Prince, the one who satisfies our hearts with His true love. As we wait for His return and the wonderful marriage we will have to Him, we easily become distracted and consumed with trinkets that are unsatisfying and fading. We easily allow other desires to take first place in our hearts. Our king wants to provide for our needs, but we are too busy to ask. Our prince is the perfect mate, and yet we become enamored with others who we only hope will understand us and meet our needs. How could we be so foolish to ignore the Lover of our souls?

His Riches and Parting Words

John, the beloved disciple, was well aware of how easy it is to be distracted from the rich treasure we have in Christ. He knew the joy of walking with Him, leaning on Him, following Him, and trusting Him. John's desire for all believers was that they remain in Christ, abiding in Him, fellowshipping with Him. He knew that true love and eternal life were found in Him alone. In Christ there is victory to overcome sin. His light breaks through our spiritual darkness. And because of Him we can come boldly before the Father with our requests. Oh, "what great love the Father has lavished on us, that we should be called children of God! And that is what we are!"[1] John wanted believers to relish the rich treasure of God's love.

Yet John was concerned that believers might lose sight of their vast riches in Christ and become enamored with valueless trinkets. He knew how easy it is to become distracted by the world. He was well aware of our tendency to stray like lost sheep, so his parting words were short but powerful. Perhaps you have read these words before, but ignored them thinking they apply to someone else. As we conclude John's unique and forthright epistle, let us take the following words personally:

1 JOHN 5:21

Dear children, keep yourselves from idols.

Idols? Really? John hasn't mentioned idols in his entire letter, and now he closes it with this instruction? That's strange! I would have closed the letter with some elegant send-off like, "And now let the True Light and the fullness of God's Love guide you upon your way!" But that's not how the apostle closed it. Instead he ended with what may seem like an out-of-place warning. Yet the more I consider this closing, the more I see its connections with the rest of his letter and the importance of this warning for all believers. He truly wants us to experience the joy of putting Christ first in our hearts.

Generally speaking, we don't consider ourselves idol worshippers. We think of them as people in ancient foreign countries who bow down to statues made of wood or bronze. We certainly don't do that kind of nonsense as civilized, churchgoing followers of Christ! Upon closer examination we find that idolatry is much more than simply worshipping silly little statues. It can actually mean anything that comes before God in our hearts. Oh. Hmm. Well now, I think this is becoming a little more personal. I'm talking to myself here, feeling a bit of conviction as God shines His light on my heart, but perhaps you are feeling His gentle tug as well.

In his book *Counterfeit Gods*, author Timothy Keller wrote,

> What is an idol? It is anything more important to you than God, anything that absorbs your heart and imagination more than God, anything you seek to give you what only God can give…
>
> An idol is whatever you look at and say, in your heart of hearts, "If I have that, then I'll feel my life has meaning, then I'll know I have value, then I'll feel significant and secure." There are many ways to describe that kind of relationship to something but perhaps the best one is *worship*.[2]

Keller's words caused me to consider what it is I value most of all in my life. What is it that I tend to worship? Is it God, or is it my family or my reputation or my work or…? Honestly, I began to realize that a good amount of my security was based on how my family acted toward me or what people thought about me. I depended on my writing projects to provide me with significance and worth.

As I carefully and thoughtfully examined what was at the core of my misplaced worship, I realized ultimately it was Me, Myself, and I at the center of my life. Oh, trust me, I was a Christian, but sadly I realized that God was not the only one I worshipped. He was not the Love of my life. It's hard for me to admit it even now. The beautiful thing is that God is continually at work in our lives; pruning us and drawing us back to Himself. He kindly reveals to us those hidden idols of the heart so that we may lovingly return to His fulfilling and warm embrace.

The Grab of Greed

One form of idolatry that can tend to pull at our affections is greed. In his letter to the Colossians Paul reminded the early believers that since they had been raised with Christ they should set their hearts and minds on things above. He instructed them to clothe themselves with compassion, kindness, humility, gentleness, and patience. He also described some old clothing to get rid of in our lives. He mentioned things like sexual immorality, impurity, lust, and evil desires. Then he added in his list of items that needed to be discarded: "greed, which is idolatry."[3] Greed—that's a little more common in our daily lives; quite a bit more than idols made of wood and bronze. Different forms of greed can affect us every day.

The temptation of greed has been grabbing at humans since the beginning of time. Greed for more knowledge enticed Eve to take that first bite of fruit from the Tree of the Knowledge of Good and Evil. Greed for approval motivated Cain to kill Abel. Greed for the best land prompted Abraham's nephew Lot to choose to live near Sodom and Gomorrah, which eventually got him in a huge mess. Throughout the Old and New Testament we read stories of greed for money, for beauty, for power, for more! And that's the essence of greed, a hunger for more, craving what will not satisfy, instead of loving the One who can truly satisfy our inner hunger. Greed is insidious and not easily recognizable.

The opposite of greed is generosity and contentment—putting your hope in God and not in things. Paul gave Timothy this healthy and heartfelt charge:

> *Godliness with contentment is great gain. For we brought nothing into the world, and we can take nothing out of it. But if we have food and clothing, we will be content with that. Those*

who want to get rich fall into temptation and a trap and into many foolish and harmful desires that plunge people into ruin and destruction. For the love of money is a root of all kinds of evil. Some people, eager for money, have wandered from the faith and pierced themselves with many griefs.

But you, man of God, flee from all this, and pursue righteousness, godliness, faith, love, endurance and gentleness. Fight the good fight of the faith. Take hold of the eternal life to which you were called when you made your good confession in the presence of many witnesses...I charge you to keep this command without spot or blame until the appearing of our Lord Jesus Christ, which God will bring about in his own time—God, the blessed and only Ruler, the King of kings and Lord of lords, who alone is immortal and who lives in unapproachable light, whom no one has seen or can see. To him be honor and might forever. Amen.

Command those who are rich in this present world not to be arrogant nor to put their hope in wealth, which is so uncertain, but to put their hope in God, who richly provides us with everything for our enjoyment. Command them to do good, to be rich in good deeds, and to be generous and willing to share. In this way they will lay up treasure for themselves as a firm foundation for the coming age, so that they may take hold of the life that is truly life.[4]

What a charge! What a perspective! What a way to fight idolatry! Put your hope in God, be rich in good deeds, be generous, and be willing to share. When we live with open hands toward others, we tend to let go of selfishness and greed and live with the kind of love John talked about earlier in this letter—the kind of love that lays down its life for others. That kind of love isn't naturally drummed up within us. That's a picture of God's love for us. His love at work in our lives transforms us from greedy people to generous people—generous with kindness and forgiveness. Let us rely on Him, keeping our hearts and minds centered on His great love.

When we turn our hearts and minds toward Him, we are reminded of His unrelenting love for us. He desires for us to embrace the joy of finding our satisfaction in Him. Richard Foster expressed it this way,

> Today the heart of God is an open wound of love. He aches over our distance and preoccupation. He mourns that we do not draw near to him. He grieves that we have forgotten him. He weeps over our obsession with muchness and manyness. He longs for our presence.[5]

Oh, how much our heavenly Father loves us! He desires for us to love Him with our whole being. John's epistle of love brings us to a choice of who we will love. Will we love the world, or will we love our loving Creator? Who gets first place?

Paul said that godliness with contentment is great gain. Godliness can be defined as a life of devotion, centered on God. Idolatry and greed lead to great loss in the lives of Christians, for we miss the rich pleasure and wonderful peace that come from a life focused on the King of kings and Lord of lords. Idolatry robs us of the genuine satisfaction that permeates our lives as a result of trusting God's love and care for us. Idolatry looks only at the happiness in the here and now and what can satisfy my temporary needs. Drawing close to God and worshipping Him keeps our focus on the eternal picture and the lasting joy that comes from knowing Him.

Jesus wanted our attention to be on laying up treasures in His kingdom rather than being consumed with worry about the things in this one. He said,

> *Do not worry about your life, what you will eat or drink; or about your body, what you will wear. Is not life more than food, and the body more than clothes? Look at the birds of the air; they do not sow or reap or store away in barns, and yet your heavenly Father feeds them. Are you not much more valuable than they? Can any one of you by worrying add a single hour to your life?*

And why do you worry about clothes? See how the flowers of the field grow. They do not labor or spin. Yet I tell you that not even Solomon in all his splendor was dressed like one of these. If that is how God clothes the grass of the field, which is here today and tomorrow is thrown into the fire, will he not much more clothe you—you of little faith? So do not worry, saying, "What shall we eat?" or "What shall we drink?" or "What shall we wear?" For the pagans run after all these things, and your heavenly Father knows that you need them. But seek first his kingdom and his righteousness, and all these things will be given to you as well. Therefore do not worry about tomorrow, for tomorrow will worry about itself. Each day has enough trouble of its own. [6]

Could it be that our worry is a form of idolatry? Surely not—I mean, worry is so popular; everyone does it. Worry certainly can't fall into the category of idolatry, now can it? Everybody has to do a little worrying, don't they? Jesus made a clear distinction between trusting God and worrying. He told us to wholeheartedly seek God's kingdom first in our lives, which is the exact opposite of idolatry. When our hearts are divided, we become distracted and we tend to forget God's great care and love for us. John wanted to make sure God's children did not become enamored with or distracted by the popular philosophies of the day. He too wanted the believers to be of one heart and mind, seeking God's kingdom first.

Entirely God's

Francois Fenelon was born in France in 1651 and was a prominent member of the court of Louis XIV. He served as the tutor of the duke of Burgundy and was highly esteemed in the church. In 1695 he was appointed as archbishop of Cambrai, and it was during this time that he became acquainted with the writings of Madame Guyon (remember her from chapter 9?) and became greatly influenced by her teaching on prayer and intimacy with God. As a result, the major themes of

Fenelon's work centered on a deep and abiding love for God. Although he suffered persecution from the established church because of his writings, he had a great influence on people's spiritual growth. His work has continued to be respected and studied even today.

Fenelon's emphasis was continually on the spiritual life as a joyful life, far from an existence filled with drudgery. He wrote,

> Those who are God's are always glad, when they are not divided, because they only want what God wants and want to do for him all that he wishes. They divest themselves of everything, and in this divesting find a hundredfold return. Peace of conscience, liberty of heart, the sweetness of abandoning ourselves in the hands of God, the joy of always seeing the light grow in our hearts, finally, freedom from the fears and insatiable desires of the times, multiply a hundredfold the happiness which the true children of God possess in the midst of their crosses, if they are faithful.[17]

Fenelon was a man sold out to God, and found great joy in a reckless abandon to Him. I believe we often get caught up in loving certain idols in our lives because we think they will satisfy us or meet a need in our lives. Whether it is a spouse or a job or house or having the "perfect" kids, we sometimes look to people or things to bring us joy and fulfillment. Certainly these things are good, but what is it that keeps us from falling into the loving arms of God and trusting Him with all of our hearts? Perhaps it is fear, or perhaps it is not really believing that He truly loves us. Fenelon goes on to address this very concept:

> What folly to fear to be too entirely God's! It is to fear to be too happy. It is to fear to love God's will in all things. It is to fear to have too much courage in the crosses which are inevitable, too much comfort in God's love, and too much detachment from the passions which make us miserable. So let us scorn earthly things, to be wholly God's. I am not saying that we should leave them absolutely, because when we are already living an honest and regulated

life, we only need to change our heart's depth in loving and
we shall do nearly the same things which we were doing…
There would be only this difference, that instead of being
devoured by our pride, by our overbearing passion, and by
the malicious criticism of the world, we shall act instead
with liberty, courage, and hope in God.

As Fenelon noted, we cannot remove all the things that draw our
hearts or compete for first place in our lives (otherwise we would be
living in a cave by ourselves), but we can change our heart attitude in
the midst of these things. May each of us as God's children experience
the joy that comes from being fully devoted to Him—a joy that comes
from the Lord and not from our circumstances! Joy in the Lord cannot be taken away from us. We can continually shift where we find our
value and strength. As we turn our worship toward God and lean into
Him, these other loves take second place. They are in our lives but don't
make up the essence of our lives.

A Jealous God?

In Exodus we read God's commandments to the Israelites:

> You must not make for yourself an idol of any kind or an image
> of anything in the heavens or on the earth or in the sea. You
> must not bow down to them or worship them, for I, the LORD
> your God, am a jealous God who will not tolerate your affec-
> tion for any other gods…I lavish unfailing love for a thousand
> generations on those who love me and obey my commands.[8]

Did you notice that nestled in this command concerning idolatry
is the reminder of God's unfailing love, which He lavishes upon us?
Because He loves us, He does not want us to fall into idolatry and fall
in love with other things.

This passage states that God is a jealous God who will not tolerate affection for any other gods. Does it bother you that God is jealous? It's easy to think of jealousy in terms of hatefulness and revenge

toward another person because that's how people often react when they are jealous. But we should not equate man's way of handling jealousy with God's. Man's character and God's character are two very different things. The word *jealous* (*qanna* in Hebrew) refers directly to the attributes of God's justice and holiness. Because He is holy He cannot tolerate sin, and because He is just He cannot tolerate the worship of other gods. The important truth is that He alone is worthy of our worship, honor, and praise. To worship anything less than Him means we are fooling ourselves and loving trinkets that cannot truly love us back.

God loves us, and He wants what is best for us. He knows that idols will never satisfy our deepest longings. They are futile imitations of the joy and hope that only He can bring. C.H. Spurgeon spoke of God's jealousy in this way: "Since he is the only God, the Creator of heaven and earth, he cannot endure that any creature of his own hands, or fiction of a creature's imagination should be thrust into his throne, and be made to wear his crown."[9] God alone has the right to be jealous. His deep love for us, His beloved people, can only lead to wanting what is pure and best for us. To worship anything other than the Lord God Himself would leave us empty and wanting. He is jealous because He loves us.

Full Circle, and Falling in Love

As we consider John's parting words, may they continually ring in our ears: "Dear children, keep yourself from idols." As odd as it may sound, this little sentence seems to sum up all that John was saying throughout his letter. His constant call was to embrace the truth of who Jesus is. He is our Source of true life. He is the one true Light of the world. He demonstrated on the cross what true love looks like. John warned believers to be careful of those who try to lead them astray. They may look like they offer life, light, and love, but don't be fooled by imitations. Have no other God before the one true God in your heart.

A.W. Tozer said, "Faith is not a once-done act, but a continuous gaze of the heart at the triune God." John urges us as children of God to remain in love with Christ. When we place our faith in Him, we do not simply walk away and say, "There you go—now I know I'm going to heaven." No, our faith is a continuous gaze of the heart at the triune God. In Him we live and move and have our being. We don't just say hello to God on Sunday mornings at church—we walk in fellowship with Him throughout all the days of our lives. He is our first and only true love.

When I think of someone who lived her life with a heavenly gaze, I think of Amy Carmichael (1867–1951). The love of God shined brightly from her devotion to the Lord. One of her confidantes had this to say about her: "Miss Carmichael was a blessing to all who came into intimate and understanding contact with her radiant life. She was the most Christlike character I ever met, and her life was the most fragrant, the most joyfully sacrificial that I have ever known."[10] Wouldn't you love to be identified by someone close to you in that manner?

Her relationship with Christ was very real. As a missionary in India she poured out her heart to the downtrodden and hurting, and she seemed to reflect the love of God in all she did. She would never take credit herself, for she recognized the power of God's love flowing through her. Like King David and the apostle John, Amy Carmichael richly embraced that God loved her with an unfailing and redeeming love, and she in turn fell in love with Him who was her all in all. Here is one of the many poems she wrote concerning her deep devotion to God and her desire for His love to flow through her:

Love Through Me, Love of God

Love through me, Love of God,
There is no love in me;
O Fire of love, light Thou the love
That burns perpetually.

Flow through me, Peace of God,
Calm river flow until
No wind can blow, no current stir
A ripple of self-will.

Shine through me, Joy of God,
Make me like Thy clear air
That Thou dost pour Thy colors through,

As though it were not there.

O blessed Love of God,
That all may taste and see
How good Thou art, once more I pray
Love through me, even me.

Think through me, thoughts of God,
That always, everywhere,
The stream that through my being flows
May homeward pass in prayer.

Think through me, thoughts of God,
And let my own thoughts be
Lost like the sand-pools on the shore
Of the eternal sea.[11]

Beloved friend, I'm so thankful you joined me on this journey through John's letter to the early believers. As you can see, God's Word is rich and full and continues to breathe into our lives today just as it did when John penned it. If we were to pull together all the wonderful lessons that we have gleaned in this letter, I suppose it would come down to this one truth: *God has lavished His great love upon us, and because of His extraordinary love, we are compelled to love Him and love others.* Let us keep our hearts and minds steadfast on the truth of who He is and what He has done for us. Christ alone—first in our hearts!

Getting Personal

ABIDING TRUTHS:

- Idolatry is anything we put before God in our hearts.
- Greed is idolatry.
- Godliness with contentment is great gain.
- Worry can be a form of idolatry.

- Seek God's kingdom first in your heart.

- Trusting God allows us to live with joy and peace.

ADDITIONAL READING: Hebrews 12

ACTION STEPS: Identifying idols

How do we recognize idols in our lives? We begin by asking the Lord to open our eyes to things or people in our lives through which we tend to find our significance. What are some areas that seem to have first place in your heart? Take some time alone with the Lord just to allow Him to teach you through His Word and through His gentle voice. Allow Him to shine His light on some of the things (even good things) that have dominated your thoughts, your worries, your time, or your money. These can be indicators of idols in our hearts. As He reveals different areas in your life that have perhaps grown into idols, confess them to God. Then spend some time worshipping and praising God for who He is and for His abundant love for you.

Thank Him that our sins are forgiven on account of His name. Guarding against idolatry is a heart shift. We change from leaning on these false idols for strength, value, and significance. Instead we lean hard into the God who loves us, and we find our security and strength in Him. Recognizing idols is a continual process in our lives. We don't just make the shift one day and say, "Done." We must realize there will always be things vying for first place in our hearts. That's why it is so important to remain in Him, worshipping Him and placing our heart and dependence back on Him no matter where we are in life.

May His love so consume your heart and mind that you seek Him as your One and Only.

Write out a prayer of praise to Him on the lines below:

_____

_____

_____

_____

_____

$\mathcal{D}$iscussion Questions

The following questions are provided for you to use along with the study of the book. You can also use the "Getting Personal" sections as catalysts for discussion.

I find it helpful to ask group participants to read the book with a highlighter in hand so they can note the passages that were particularly meaningful. It always enriches the study to hear what women have highlighted and discuss why that particular passage is meaningful to them. (For more tips to help you lead a discussion group, please go to my website for a free download: www.PositiveLifePrinciples.com.)

I'm thankful you have chosen to study this book. May God bless you as you grow to love Him more.

Start Your Own "Positive Woman Connection" Discussion Group or Bible Study

In Dallas I lead several lunchtime Bible studies called "The Positive Woman Connection." Women of all ages and denominations join together around the lunch table to listen to the teaching of God's Word as well as enjoy food and fellowship together. I encourage you to use this book about God's love to invite women to study and grow together. You can study one or two chapters per session. A hearty discussion always enhances your time together and develops a deeper bond between the women who are at your study.

Please feel free to e-mail me and let me know you are starting a Positive Woman Connection (Karol@Karolladd.com). I'd be happy to share ideas and principles we have gleaned from our groups here in Dallas. As a leader, your most important preparation for leading a group study is prayer. One of the principles we learned in this book throughout our journey through 1 John is the principle of remaining and abiding in Him. As you look to Christ to help you teach and to bless the women in your study, you will be fruitful indeed. Walk together with the Lord as you lead this study and allow His abundant love to flow through you.

Part One: Living in the Light of God's Great Love

Chapter One: Complete Joy

1. Why is it important for us to know the truth about Christ?

2. What significance does the term "Word of Life" hold in describing Jesus, and what does it mean to you personally?

3. Name at least one common bond you share with your current group of friends.

4. When is a time you would say you have experienced true fellowship with other believers?

5. In what way do you see yourself in partnership with God to carry out His work here on the earth?

Chapter Two: Light Up Your Life

1. In what ways are the characteristics of light representative of the character of God?

2. Why is it important to recognize we are sinful?

3. Why is confession of your sins important in your relationship with God?

4. What does it mean to you personally to know God is faithful and just?

5. In what ways does your life show evidence that you live in Him?

Part Two: Doing the Will of God

Chapter Three: The New and Improved You

1. Which fruits of God's Spirit are abundantly evident in your own life?

2. In what ways was Christ's love revolutionary?

3. How are people who live with continual hatred and bitterness blinded in their own eyes?

4. In what ways does God's Word help us to walk in the light?

5. Which of the three types of people mentioned in 1 John (children, fathers, young men) can you relate to in regard to where you are in your Christian walk?

Chapter Four: Who Do You Love?

1. What does it mean to "love the world"?

2. What are some of the temptations in our culture that tend to encourage a love for the world?

3. How do we actively and consistently set our affections on things above?

4. How would you describe the love for God in contrast to the love for the world?

5. In what ways would you say you are rich toward God?

6. In practical terms, how can we combat the lust of the eyes and the constant desire for more?

Part Three: Being Beautiful

Chapter Five: Fulfilling Fellowship

1. What kinds of false teachings are prevalent in today's culture, and how are they contrary to the truth?

2. How would it be possible for a person to be ashamed when Christ returns?

3. In what ways does our obedience demonstrate our relationship with Christ?

4. In a practical sense, how can we become gloves and allow God to work through us?

5. How do you sense the Holy Spirit's presence in your own life?

Chapter Six: Lavishly Loved by Him

1. Why is it that we so easily forget how much God loves us? How is God's *hesed* love different from the love between people?

2. How does it change you as a person to know that His love is generous, unrelenting, and faithful?

3. Is it possible for us to love the people in our lives with a God-type of love?

4. Because of His love for you, how does that build your anticipation for the glorious day when we will see Him face-to-face?

Part Four: Recognizing Real Faith

Chapter Seven: Bold Confidence

1. Why is hatred so destructive to others as well as ourselves?

2. How does God's perfect love cast out fear in your life?

3. In what ways has God led you to sacrificially love others?

4. Are there any new ways God is prompting you to reach out and love, help, or forgive others?

5. What difference does the Holy Spirit make in your life as you relate to others?

Chapter Eight: Don't Be Fooled

1. Have you ever been intrigued or confused by false teachings, or have you ever known someone who has?

2. Why is it important to study the claims Jesus made about Himself?

3. How does listening to the truth of God's Word affect our lives?

4. Why is it tempting to listen to the world's point of view rather than the Bible?

5. What encouragement do you find from knowing that the One who is in you is greater than the one who is in the world?

Part Five: Loving Because We Are Loved

Chapter Nine: Organic Love

1. Although the world may give us examples of what it calls "true love," what example does John give us?

2. If you are struggling to love a brother or sister in Christ, where can you go for help?

3. In your opinion, why do we often think of seeking God's help as the last resort instead of our first resource?

4. What is it about God's love that most intrigues and inspires you?

5. Why do you think it is so difficult for us to trust God's love and be confident in His salvation?

6. In what ways does this chapter inspire you to reach out and demonstrate God's love to others?

Chapter Ten: God's Family Portrait

1. As believers, how can people identify us as God's family?

2. What are some ways that Christians do not provide a good family portrait in today's culture?

3. Why is it difficult for people to accept the fact that Jesus is the Way?

4. How does your faith in God give you victory in this world?

5. Why do you think John wanted to make sure we knew that God's commands are not burdensome?

Part Six: Knowing We Are His

Chapter Eleven: Utterly and Eternally Secure

1. How does it build your confidence to know you have the certainty of eternal life?

2. In what ways does it change your prayer life to know that if you pray according to His will, He hears you?

3. When you face temptations to sin, what strength does it give you to know you have victory over sin?

4. Knowing you are a child of God—how does that affect the way you relate to God and to others?

5. Since you know that Jesus is the One True God, in what ways do you honor Him and show Him adoration in your daily life?

Chapter Twelve: First Place in Our Hearts

1. What are some of the idols that seem prevalent in our society today, especially for women?

2. How can we change our affection in the midst of our lives right now?

3. Why is God a jealous God? Why do you think it bothers some people to hear that He is jealous?

4. What makes it so easy to become distracted from thinking about and remembering His great love for us?

5. How can you be more consistent in worshipping and praising God each day?

Closing Prayer

As you close your study together, I encourage you to pray the prayer on the next page, the prayer that Paul prayed for the Ephesian church. It is a prayer that believers would embrace God's love in a deeper and richer sense in their lives. Allow this to be your personal prayer as well as a prayer you pray for your family and friends. The blanks are provided for you to personalize the prayer for whomever God lays on your heart.

*I kneel before the Father, from whom every family
in heaven and on earth derives its name.*

*I pray that out of his glorious riches he may strengthen
_____ with power through his Spirit in _____
inner being, so that Christ may dwell in _____ hearts
through faith. And I pray that _____, being
rooted and established in love, may have power, together
with all the Lord's holy people, to grasp how wide and long
and high and deep is the love of Christ, and to know this
love that surpasses knowledge—that _____
may be filled to the measure of all the fullness of God.*

*Now to him who is able to do immeasurably more than all
we ask or imagine, according to his power that is at work
within us, to him be glory in the church and in Christ Jesus
throughout all generations, for ever and ever! Amen.*[1]

Keep shining His light, my friend! Allow His love to flow through you to change the world around you. You are not alone. May God's Spirit continue to lead you and guide you and light your path each step of the way.

$\mathscr{K}$eys for Memorizing Scripture

Marvelous Memory

It's amazing what our minds can do! Not too long ago I read a short biography about a godly woman and gifted hymn writer named Frances Ridley Havergal. Born in 1836, she was to Great Britain what Fanny Crosby was to the United States. You are probably familiar with some of her beloved hymns, such as "Take My Life and Let It Be" and "Like a River Glorious." Although she faced many challenges in her life, both physically and circumstantially, her faith remained strong, and her foundation was in God's Word. She kept her daily quiet time with the Lord with devoted discipline, but what fascinated me the most about this woman was her commitment to Bible memory.

After Frances passed away in 1879, her sister revealed that Frances had memorized all of the Gospels and epistles, as well as Isaiah (her favorite book), the Psalms, the minor prophets, and Revelation! [1] Wait a minute—can someone really do that? It is interesting to note that in Jesus' day, many Jewish boys had memorized the Torah (the first five books of the Old Testament) by the age of 12!

Now I know you are most likely thinking, *But I can't even remember where I put my car keys...how can I memorize Scripture?* You are not alone. Most people cringe when they hear the words "Scripture memory," and they feel like failures as they reflect on their few futile attempts to memorize Scripture in the past. I hope I can shine a bright ray of hope into your less-than-positive view of Bible memorization and help you see the opportunity to hide God's Word in your heart in a fresh new way.

Why Memorize?

Recently I was in a meeting. Sitting next to me was a Bible seminary student. He said he had almost lost his motivation to memorize Scripture because anytime he needs a verse, he just finds it on the Internet. If he can remember several words or a phrase, then he can find the verse in a split second using his smartphone. Scripture memory—who needs it in today's information-at-your-fingertips world?

My response is, we need it because we need God's Word ready and available in our minds. In his first epistle, John addressed the young men: "I write to you, young men, because you are strong, and the word of God lives in you, and you have overcome the evil one." [2] The word of God lived in the young men! And how powerful that word was in helping them overcome the evil one and staying strong! Now I can speak for myself—I need strength in overcoming temptations and discouragements. I need the strength and power of God's word in me, reminding me of His truth.

How did Jesus fight the temptation of the devil in the wilderness? He recalled Scripture. He didn't say, "Hold on while I look up a helpful passage for that temptation." No, He was ready with the Word of God, which Paul called the "sword of the Spirit." Paul also reminds us in Colossians to "let the word of Christ dwell in you richly." [3] In Philippians 4:8 we are challenged to let our minds think on what is true, noble, right, pure, lovely, admirable, excellent, and praiseworthy. In Romans 12:2 we are told to be transformed by the renewing of our minds. Yes, our minds steer us in a variety of directions, so a mind that is focused on the living Word of God is a mind that is able to have victory over the daily battles life brings.

We allow our minds to absorb quite a bit of data each day, so why shouldn't we be deliberate about dwelling on His Word and inviting it to be a rich part of our very being? For me, Bible memory has made a dramatic difference in my life. I'm able to comfort loved ones. I am able to encourage a friend. I always have a good thought to write in a note or share with someone during a challenging time. I teach and speak with more power as a result of memorizing Scripture. I live with a greater confidence day in and day out as God's Word reassures me of His love and presence through my struggles.

What's the Key?

We all learn a little differently, but there are certain tried and true methods of memorization that work for most people. The following tips have helped me, as well as many others, be successful. Now I want you to know I'm not a brilliant scholar with a gazillion degrees to my name. I'm just a regular, normal, everyday person, and I've now memorized several books (yes, books) of the Bible and plan to do more. It's possible! You can join me on this joyful journey of memorizing the Bible with hope and not frustration. Believe that God has equipped you with the capacity to do it and take one step at a time. Here are my keys to success.

Pictures. Our minds can hold onto pictures more readily and easily than words. When I begin to memorize a verse, I draw a picture for each word. The crazier or more ridiculous the picture, the better. For instance, I John 5 begins, "Everyone who believes that Jesus is the Christ is born of God." So I drew a big "E" with a bunch of faces around it to represent "everyone." For the word "who" I drew an owl (trust me, my drawing is pitiful, but I at least know what it is), and for "believes" I drew a bumblebee with leaves (like from a tree) as wings. Remember, the crazier the picture the better. For the word "that" I drew a flat hat (that's the picture I always draw for the word "that"). My symbol for Jesus is the cross, and for Christ it is the crown of thorns. For the word "born" I draw a newborn baby, and for God I draw a cloud with a "G" in the center. Get the picture of what I'm saying?

Repetition. Pictures may seem like fun, but repetition and review form the most powerful key to retaining information. Write the verse (plus pictures) on index cards and place the cards throughout your house so you will see them several times a day. Review the verse before you go to bed. Then in the morning, try to say it by memory. You will most likely stumble a little bit and need to look back. Don't let that discourage you.

Repeat the verse over for several days. Look for opportunities to share it in conversations. Speak it out loud. Often I review memory work while I'm exercising. When I'm at my own house, I say the memory work out loud because it is sealed in my brain as I speak it and hear it. Review your past memory work on a regular basis. I have a few passages I recite every day, and others I review weekly. I keep a notebook divided into different days of the week with the printed verses so I can review memorized verses for accuracy.

Accountability. Find someone who values Scripture memory like you do, perhaps someone in your Bible-study group. Even if your accountability partner doesn't want to memorize Scripture, you can still ask them to hold you accountable and listen to you recite. I encourage you to print out the verse or bring your Bible when you recite to one another so you can check for accuracy. Set a regular meeting time each month to get together and recite. Commit to meet with each other, and make it a priority. Trust me, it's easy to come up with excuses and let it fall by the wayside. Accountability is a vital key to staying diligent in this important endeavor.

You. There are certain physical activities you can do to encourage a stronger capacity for Scripture memory. Exercise increases oxygen flow to your brain. It is believed it may also enhance the effects of helpful brain chemicals and protect brain cells. When I go over my memory work while I'm working out, I find that it is much easier to recall. The rhythm of walking or running or elliptical training seems to help, and I stay more alert. Plus it gets my mind off the challenges of working out.

Getting enough sleep is also important. Sleep deprivation diminishes our brain's ability to work at full capacity. Studies now show that sleep is necessary for memory consolidation, with the key memory-enhancing activity occurring during the deepest stages of sleep.[4] So take care of yourself while you are passionately pursuing His Word.

Where Do You Begin?

Perhaps you noticed that the first letters of the keys I gave you created an acrostic—PRAY. Begin with prayer, asking the Lord to help you. The book of 1 John tells us that we walk in fellowship (partnership) with God. It is His Word, and He will help you hold on to it. Pray for guidance as to how your mind works best, and pray for Him to show you which Scripture passages you need to memorize. As you prayerfully choose, I would encourage you to start with a passage or verses with which you are fairly familiar or that are particularly meaningful to you. Get the tools you need, such as index cards and colorful markers and an accountability partner. Stay diligent! I know you will experience lasting rewards as you hide His Word in your heart.

Notes

Chapter 1—Complete Joy

1. Story used by permission of Greg and Leigh Anne Bland, www.prfellowship.com.
2. Mark 10:35-40.
3. Luke 9:51-56.
4. Hebrews 10:24-25.
5. John Phillips, *Exploring the Epistles of John* (Grand Rapids, MI: Kregel Publications, 2003), p. 30.
6. John 15:5.
7. http://firstfridaywomen.com.

Chapter 2—Light Up Your Life

1. James 1:17.
2. Ephesians 5:1-5,8-14.
3. Colossians 1:22.
4. Matthew 5:3.
5. Warren W. Wiersbe, *Be Real* (Colorado Springs, CO: David C. Cook, 1972), p. 38.
6. John MacArthur, *The MacArthur Bible Commentary* (Nashville, TN: Thomas Nelson Publishers, 2005), pp. 1951-2.

Chapter 3—The New and Improved You

1. Matthew 7:15-20.
2. Galatians 5:19-21.
3. Galatians 5:22-25.
4. John 13:34-35.
5. Jim Eckhardt, "Hungering for Holiness" Riverside, CA: Haven Ministries, 1981), pp. 4-5. Eckhardt is quoting 2 Corinthians 5:17.

6. Psalm 19:8,12-14.

7. Mark 10:14.

8. Psalm 119:9,11.

9. John Calvin/Matthew Henry, "1, 2, 3 John," *The Crossway Classic Commentaries* (Wheaton, IL: Crossway Publishers, 1998), p. 37.

10. Irenaeus, *Adversus Haereses,* Book III; Irenaeus mentions the anecdote about Polycarp in *Adv. Haer.*, III.3.4.

11. http://gospeldrivendisciples.blogspot.com/2011/05/cerinthus.html.

Chapter 4—Who Do You Love?

1. *More Gathered Gold,* ed. John Blanchard (Hertfordshire, England: Evangelical Press, 1986), p. 341.

2. *More Gathered Gold*, p. 343.

3. Colossians 3:1-3.

4. Colossians 2:2-3.

5. *More Gathered Gold,* p. 342.

6. www.providencedallas.com/bulletins/5.1.11.pdf.

7. Luke 12:15:21 NLT.

8. John Calvin / Matthew Henry, "1, 2, 3 John," *The Crossway Classic Commentaries* (Wheaton, IL: Crossway Publishers, 1998), p. 39.

9. Psalm 34:5 NLT.

10. Psalm 121.

11. Elisabeth Elliot, *Shadow of the Almighty* (New York: Harper and Row, 1958), p. 108.

12. Matt Redman, *The Unquenchable Worshipper* (Ventura, CA: Gospel Light Publications, 2001), p. 1.

13. John 8:23-26 NLT.

Chapter 5—Fulfilling Fellowship

1. Myra Brooks Welch, 1921.

2. Lilly Walters, "The One Hand Typing and Keyboarding Manual: With Personal Motivational Messages from Others Who Have Overcome!" © 2003 Lilly Walters; for more on one-hand typing, see www.aboutonehandtyping.com.

3. C.H. Spurgeon, *Morning and Evening* (Ross-shire, Scotland: Christian Focus Publications, 1994), August 4.

4. Spurgeon, August 4.

5. Matthew 5:14-16.

6. John 15:5.

7. John 15:9-10.

8. Ephesians 5:18 NKJV.

9. John 14:26.

10. Colossians 2:18-19.

11. Nathanael Emmons, quoted in *More Gathered Gold,* ed. John Blanchard (Hertfordshire, England: Evangelical Press, 1986), p. 214.

12. John 14:15 NASB.

13. John 14:15-17.

14. Psalm 37:23-24 NLT.

Chapter 6—Lavishly Loved by Him

1. You can read Beth's blog at www.bgotwalt.wordpress.com.

2. Psalm 36:5-9.

3. Psalm 63:2-3 NLT.

4. Psalm 103:11-13.

5. Psalm 106:1.

6. Hosea 2:19-20.

7. Jeremiah 9:23-24.

8. 1 Corinthians 13:4-8.

9. See Romans 5:8.

10. www.basarchive.org/sample/bswbBrowse.asp?PubID=BSBR&Volume=19&Issue=6&ArticleID=7.

11. Chip Ingram, *God: As He Longs for You to See Him* (Grand Rapids, MI: Baker Books, 2004), p. 181.

12. Ephesians 3:18-19.

13. Romans 8:38-39.

14. Romans 8:15-16.

15. John Phillips, *Exploring the Epistles of John* (Grand Rapids, MI: Kregel Publications, 2003), p. 88.

16. Thomas Watson, as quoted in *More Gathered Gold*, ed. John Blanchard (Hertfordshire, England: Evangelical Press, 1986), p.3.

17. John 1:10.

18. Revelation 19–22.

19. Philippians 3:20-21.

20. Sarah Young, *40 Days with Jesus* (Nashville, TN: Thomas Nelson, 2010) p. 11.

21. 2 Corinthians 5:21.

22. Galatians 2:16 NLT.

23. 1 Corinthians 10:13 NLT.

24. L.B. Cowman, comp., *Streams in the Desert* (Grand Rapids, MI: Zondervan Publishing, 1996), pp. 240-241.

25. Ingram, p. 65.

Chapter 7—Bold Confidence

1. C.S. Lewis, *The Four Loves* (New York: Harcourt-Brace, 1960).

2. John 3:19-21.

3. Matthew 5:21–22.

4. John 15:19.

5. John 10:11.

6. John 15:13.

7. Kenneth S. Wuest, *Wuest's Word Studies from the Greek New Testament for the English Reader* (Grand Rapids, MI: Eerdmans, 1979), 1 Jn. 3:16.

8. John Phillips, *Exploring the Epistles of John* (Grand Rapids, MI: Kregel Publications, 2003), p. 111.

9. Philippians 2:3-11.

10. Luke 23:34.

11. Brennan Manning, *The Wisdom of Tenderness* (New York: Harper One, 2002), p. 145.

12. Paul Boese, 1668–1738.

13. Allison Bottke, *Setting Boundaries with Difficult People* (Eugene, OR: Harvest House Publishers, 2011), pp. 30,31.

14. John 15:7-12.

15. John Calvin, Thomas Henry L. Parker, *The Epistles of Paul the Apostle to the Galatians, Ephesians, and Philippians* (Grand Rapids, MI: Eerdmans, 1996), p. 106.

16. Lyrics written in 1907 by Henry J. van Dyke (1852–1933).

Chapter 8—Don't Be Fooled

1. Cerinthus, a false teacher at the time of John's writings, used arguments such as these to try to lead believers astray. This is a fictional dramatization from a novel about the apostle John: Tim LaHaye and Jerry Jenkins, *John's Story: The Last Eyewitness* (New York: Putnam Praise, 2006), pp. 39,40.

2. 1 Timothy 4:1-2 NLT.

3. 1 Timothy 4:13 NLT.

4. Colossians 2:9.

5. John 20:30-31.

6. John 6:35.

7. John 8:12.

8. John 10:7-9.

9. John 10:11-14.

10. John 11:25.

11. John 14:6.

12. John 15:1,5.

13. John 2:1-11.

14. John 4:46-54.

15. John 5:1-23.

16. John 6:1-15.

17. John 6:16-21.

18. John 9:1-41.

19. John 11:1-57.

20. If you want to talk with someone personally about a relationship with Christ, call 1-888-Need-Him. Or go online to www.chataboutJesus.com.

21. Ephesians 4:17-19.

22. Romans 1:21-25.

Chapter 9—Organic Love

1. To learn more about Gospel for Asia you can go to www.gfa.org.

2. 2 Corinthians 4:6-7.

3. Madame Jeanne Guyon, *Experiencing the Depths of Jesus Christ,* ed. Gene Edwards (Goleta, CA: Christian Books, 1975), p. 10.

4. John 13:35.

5. Ephesians 1:13-14.

6. Revelation 2:4-5.

Chapter 10—God's Family Portrait

1. 1 John 3:23.

2. Matthew 11:30.

3. John 16:33 NASB.

4. Ephesians 6:16.

5. Romans 8:31-39.

6. Colossians 2:13-15.

7. www.uplink.com.au/lawlibrary/Documents/Docs/Doc51.html.

8. http://en.wikipedia.org/wiki/Credible_witness.

9. Matthew 3:16-17.

10. Luke 9:35.

11. John 10:9-10.

12. L. Richards and L.O. Richards, *The Teacher's Commentary* (Wheaton, IL: Victor Books, 1987), p. 1060.

Chapter 11—Utterly and Eternally Secure

1. www.thearda.com/quickstats/qs_155.asp.

2. www.usatoday.com/news/religion/2008-12-18-saved-heaven_N.htm.

3. Colossians 1:27.

4. Ephesians 2:8-10.

5. Matthew 7:9-11.

6. Psalm 66:16-20 NLT.

7. Wiersbe, *Be Real* (Colorado Springs, CO: David C. Cook, 1972), p. 181.

8. C.H. Spurgeon, *Morning and Evening,* Morning, September 9.

9. Psalm 50:14-15,23 NLT.

10. 1 John 3:21-22.

11. 1 Corinthians 11:27-30.

12. Acts 5:1-11.

13. Mark 3:29.

14. Galatians 6:1-2.

15. Oswald Chambers, *Not Knowing Where* (Grand Rapids, MI: Discovery House, 1989), p. 110.

16. Colossians 3:3.

Chapter 12—First Place in Our Hearts

1. 1 John 3:1.

2. Timothy Keller, *Counterfeit Gods* (New York: Dutton Adult, 2009), p. xviii.

3. See Colossians 3:1-5.

4. 1 Timothy 6:6-19.

5. Richard Foster, *Prayer: Finding the Heart's True Home* (New York: Harper One, 1992), p. 1.

6. Matthew 6:25-34.

7. Francois Fenelon, *Christian Perfection* (Minneapolis, MN: Bethany House, 1976).

8. Exodus 20:4-6 NLT.

9. www.spurgeon.org/sermons/0502.htm.

10. www.gfamissions.org/missionary-biographies/carmichael-amy-1867-1951.html.

11. Amy Carmichael, "Love Through Me" (poem), in *Mountain Breezes: The Collected Poems of Amy Carmichael* (Fort Washington, PA: CLC Publications, 1999), p. 248. Used by permission.

Discussion Questions

1. Ephesians 3:14-21.

Keys for Memorizing Scripture

1. Warren W. Wiersbe, *50 People Every Christian Should Know* (Grand Rapids, MI: Baker Books, 2009), p. 159.

2. 1 John 2:14.

3. Colossians 3:16 NKJV.

4. www.helpguide.org/life/improving_memory.htm.

$\mathscr{A}$bout the Author

Karol Ladd is known as the "Positive Lady." Her unique gift of encouraging women from the truths of God's Word, as well as her enthusiasm and joy, is evident in both her speaking and her writing.

Karol is the bestselling author of over 25 books, including *The Power of a Positive Mom, A Woman's Passionate Pursuit of God* (book and DVD), and *A Woman's Secret to Confident Living* (book and DVD). She is a gifted Bible teacher and popular speaker to women's organizations, church groups, and corporate events across the nation. Karol is also a frequent guest on radio and television, sharing a message of joy and strength found in the Lord. Her most valued role is that of wife to Curt and mother to daughters Grace and Joy.

Visit her website at www.PositiveLifePrinciples.com for daily doses of encouragement and more information on how you can start your own Positive Woman Connection Bible Study.

Also by Karol Ladd

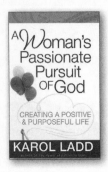

A Woman's Passionate Pursuit of God
Creating a Positive and Purposeful Life
(book and DVD)

As you explore Paul's intriguing letter to the Philippians with popular author and speaker Karol Ladd, you'll learn to live intentionally as you face life's daily challenges. Most important, you'll be helped to understand God's Word and His plans for your life and say more and more, "Father, I want what You want."

Filled with inspiring true-life stories, practical steps, and study questions, this book is perfect for personal quiet times, a book club pick, or a group Bible study.

It's complemented by the DVD version, offering six 30-minute sessions from Karol, a helpful leader's guide, and discussion questions. *Excellent for small-group or church class study.*

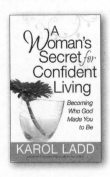

A Woman's Secret for Confident Living
Becoming Who God Made You to Be
(book and DVD)

Bestselling author Karol Ladd shares powerful truths from the book of Colossians to help you make a vital shift in perspective. Knowing Christ and His greatness, and knowing who you are in Him, sets you on an exciting path to living—not in self-confidence, but *God*-confidence. You'll be helped to

- get rid of negative and self-defeating thoughts
- cultivate your potential, because you're valuable to Him
- shine with joy and assurance of what you bring to the world

Includes questions to bring depth and dimension to individual or group study.

In the complementary DVD version, Karol digs transforming truth out of the Scriptures in six positive, inspiring sessions such as "Transform Your Thinking," "Grow in Christ," and "Strengthen Your Relationships." *Helpful leader's guide included for group use.*

Pursuing God in the Quiet Places

Every aspect of God's nature and character is an encouragement and a reason to be grateful. The more you know about Him, the more you will experience His joy.

Revel in His presence, character, and love in this fresh gathering of intimate devotions. Each meditation illumines a character quality of God from the Scriptures, igniting praise and admiration for the One who cares so much about you.

As you come to know and understand Him better, your heart and life will overflow with love—His love—throughout your day.

Allison Bottke Helps You Tackle
Tough Relationships with SANITY

S = Stop enabling, stop blaming yourself, and stop the flow of money
A = Assemble a support group
N = Nip excuses in the bud
I = Implement rules and boundaries
T = Trust your instincts
Y = Yield everything to God

Allison shows you how to put these six steps to work in...

Setting Boundaries® with Difficult People
Six Steps to SANITY for Challenging Relationships

We all have at least one difficult person we just can't seem to mesh with. Perhaps they're too demanding, never satisfied with our efforts, or just plain ornery.

What can we do? We can—and must—set realistic boundaries that will decrease our own stress level and may even benefit that difficult person. Whether you're struggling with a friend, relative, coworker, boss, neighbor, or just an acquaintance, Allison Bottke can help you establish those necessary boundaries to bring sanity back into your life.

Setting Boundaries® with Your Adult Children
Six Steps to Hope and Healing for Struggling Parents

In spite of a mom and dad's best efforts, their most heartfelt prayers, and a loving environment, some kids never successfully make the transition to independent-functioning adulthood. The result is pain for the parents—and often the repeated cycle of "starting over" that ends only days or weeks later in yet another failure.

After struggling with her own adult son, author Allison Bottke offers a tough-love approach to parenting adult children that focuses on setting you free from the repeated pain of your adult child's broken promises, lies, and deception. Here's hope and a solid, workable plan to make your future different—and *better*.

> *"Powerful...I pray that it will be a tool for healing in*
> *many families. Allison Bottke has done an extraordinary job!"*

Carol Kent, author of *When I Lay My Isaac Down*